Shelley's
First Love

Shelley's First Love

DESMOND HAWKINS

/370367

KYLE CATHIE
ARCHON BOOKS

First published in Great Britain in 1992 by
Kyle Cathie Limited
3 Vincent Square, London SW1P 2LX
and in the United States of America by Archon Books Inc
925 Sherman Avenue, Hamden, Connecticut 06514

British ISBN 1 85626 048 8
US ISBN 0 208 02363–1

Desmond Hawkins is hereby identified as the author of this work in
accordance with Section 77 of the Copyright, Designs and Patents Act 1988.

A CIP catalogue record for this book is available from the British Library.

Typeset by DP Photosetting, Aylesbury, Bucks
Printed and bound in Great Britain by
Butler & Tanner Ltd, Frome and London

The publication of this volume has been aided by a grant from
The Carl and Lily Pforzheimer Foundation, Inc

CONTENTS

List of Illustrations

Thomas Grove (Harriet's father, Shelley's uncle). Portrait by George Romney, 1788.

John Grove (Shelley's London host at 49 Lincoln's Inn Fields). Portrait by Margaret Carpenter, 1852.

Ferne House, 1850, as the young Groves would have known it. The original sixteenth-century building was demolished and the family seat rebuilt in 1809–11.

Harriet Grove, c.1808–9: a pencil sketch attributed to Elizabeth Shelley – 'Elizabeth has sent me my picture' (Harriet's diary, 29 August 1809).

An unfinished oil portrait of Shelley c.1822 by Amelia Curran.

Charles Henry Grove: close companion of Shelley in London, 1811, and later rector of Sedgehill in south-west Wiltshire.

Hellen Shelley in 1862. She maintained a lifelong relationship with her Wiltshire cousins.

Field Place, the Shelleys' residence near Horsham in Sussex.

Shelley's diary, 15 January 1810: '30 copies of Zastrozzi to come – not to forget Harriet'.

Harriet's diary, 28 March 1810: 'Bysshe has sent C. & me Zastrozzi as it is come out'.

Shelley's diary, 1 March 1810: 'Parcel to Harriet'.

Harriet's diary, 5 March 1810: 'Most agreeably surprised by receiving a Parcel & letter from my Greatest Friend'.

'St Irvyne' (Hill Place, near Horsham): a scene of romantic memories for Shelley and Harriet Grove.

Cwm Elan: Thomas Grove's estate in Wales, where Shelley stayed in 1811 and again, with his first wife, in 1812. Painting by R. Eustace Tickell.

ACKNOWLEDGMENTS

It must be nearly ten years since I first visited the Pforzheimer Library in New York and made the personal acquaintance of the editor of *Shelley and his Circle*, Donald Reiman, and the associate editor, Doucet Fischer, who responded most cordially to my interest in Harriet Grove's diaries, which are part of the Carl H. Pforzheimer collection of Shelleyana now located in the New York Public Library, and published in volume two of *Shelley and his Circle*. From them, and latterly from Carl H. Pforzheimer III, I have received much encouragement and support in the preparation of this book. For the reproduction here of two pages from Harriet's 1810 diary I acknowledge formally the Carl H. Pforzheimer Shelley and his Circle Collection, the New York Public Library Astor, Lenox and Tilden Foundations. For permission to reproduce the Romney portrait of Thomas Grove I am indebted to the Detroit Institute of Arts, and I am most grateful to Timothy Heneage (a descendant of Harriet Grove's) for permission to publish the pencil portrait of Harriet. The portrait of Shelley by Amelia Curran is reproduced courtesy of the National Portrait Gallery. The painting of Cwm Elan by R. Eustace Tickell is reproduced in his book *The Vale of Nantgwyllt* (London, 1894).

For other illustrations deriving from the family photo albums of the Groves I owe a special debt of gratitude to the late Mrs Pleydell-Railstone (a granddaughter of Kate Grove); and more recently to her daughter, the late Patricia Chichester and her husband Desmond Chichester. Their generosity and fortitude in coping with my importunities over the years are such that most researchers can only dream of. I am similarly indebted to Michael Carey, the Grove family solicitor, who first steered the substantial remnants of the Grove archive into my hands.

In the preparation of the text I have been helped by St Bartholomew's Hospital archivist; Guildford Local Studies Library;

the Ministry of Defence, Admiralty, for naval records; the Wiltshire Record Office (Andrew Crookston); the Horsham Museum; and Brian Lawrence of Powys County Library. Malvina Tribe has typed every page with her exemplary care; and I have had the pleasure of renewing my professional association with Brenda Thomson (editor) and Robert Updegraff (designer). The last word is reserved for my publisher, Kyle Cathie, whose unflinching confidence was worth the equivalent of an armoured division to my morale.

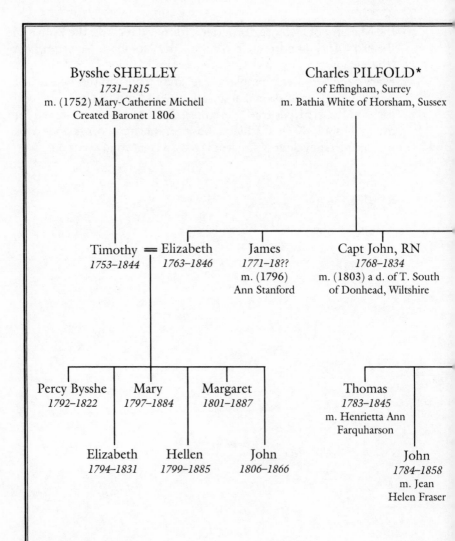

Bysshe SHELLEY
1731–1815
m. (1752) Mary-Catherine Michell
Created Baronet 1806

Charles PILFOLD*
of Effingham, Surrey
m. Bathia White of Horsham, Sussex

Timothy = Elizabeth
1753–1844　*1763–1846*

James
1771–18??
m. (1796)
Ann Stanford

Capt John, RN
1768–1834
m. (1803) a d. of T. South
of Donhead, Wiltshire

Percy Bysshe
1792–1822

Mary
1797–1884

Margaret
1801–1887

Thomas
1783–1845
m. Henrietta Ann
Farquharson

Elizabeth
1794–1831

Hellen
1799–1885

John
1806–1866

John
1784–1858
m. Jean
Helen Fraser

*Charles Pilfold had a brother whose daughter married Thomas Charles Medwin, Steward of the Duke of Norfolk and father of Thomas Medwin (1788–1869), biographer and second cousin of Percy Bysshe Shelley. Bathia White's relatives included Mrs Shelley's aunt, Lady Poole (daughter of Thomas White), who virtually adopted Elizabeth Pilfold during her childhood (Medwin's *Life of Shelley*).

FIGURE 1 **The Principal Relationships Linking the Families of Shelley, Grove**

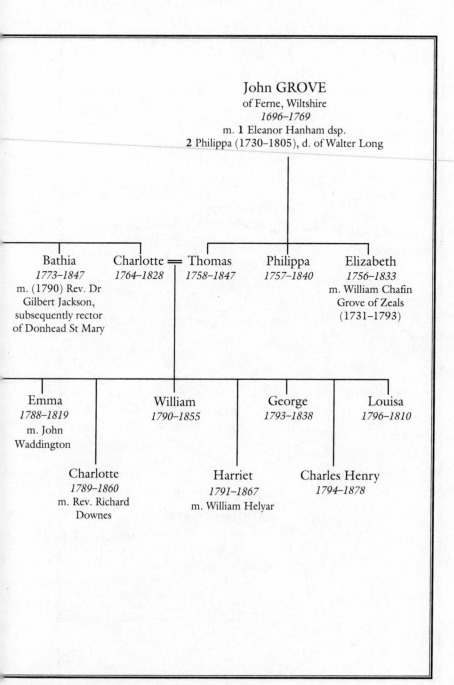

John GROVE
of Ferne, Wiltshire
1696–1769
m. 1 Eleanor Hanham dsp.
2 Philippa (1730–1805), d. of Walter Long

Bathia
1773–1847
m. (1790) Rev. Dr
Gilbert Jackson,
subsequently rector
of Donhead St Mary

Charlotte ══ **Thomas**
1764–1828   *1758–1847*

Philippa
1757–1840

Elizabeth
1756–1833
m. William Chafin
Grove of Zeals
(1731–1793)

Emma
1788–1819
m. John
Waddington

William
1790–1855

George
1793–1838

Louisa
1796–1810

Charlotte
1789–1860
m. Rev. Richard
Downes

Harriet
1791–1867
m. William Helyar

Charles Henry
1794–1878

and Pilfold at the Beginning of the Nineteenth Century.

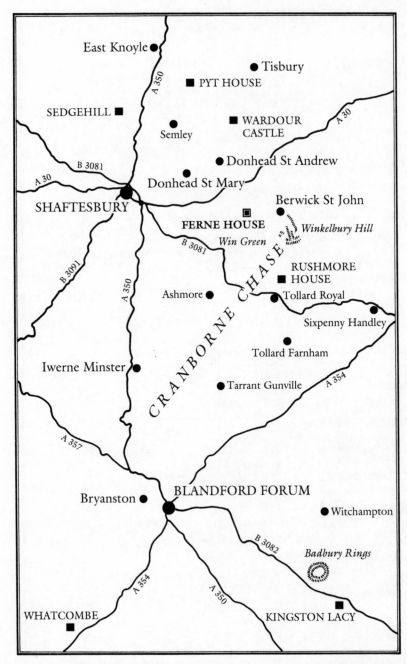

FIGURE 2 **Ferne and Its Vicinity on the Wiltshire–Dorset Border.**

PRINCIPAL CHARACTERS

The Shelleys

Timothy Shelley MP (1753–1844) of Field Place, Sussex; son of Sir
 Bysshe Shelley and father of the poet, Percy Bysshe Shelley.
Mrs Shelley (*née* Elizabeth Pilfold, 1763–1846).
Percy Bysshe (1792–1822), their eldest son.
Elizabeth (1794–1831), their eldest daughter.
For other children, see Fig. 1.

The Groves

Thomas Grove senior (1758–1847) of Ferne, Wiltshire.
Mrs Grove (*née* Charlotte Pilfold, 1764–1828).
Thomas Grove junior (1783–1845), their eldest son and heir,
 married Henrietta Ann Farquharson.
Harriet Grove (1791–1867), a daughter, married William Helyar.
Charlotte Grove (1783–1860), a daughter, married Rev. Richard
 Downes.
John Grove (1784–1858), second son and eventual heir; a surgeon,
 residing at 49 Lincoln's Inn Fields; thought to be an unsuccessful
 suitor for Elizabeth Shelley.
William Grove (1790–1855), a son; a naval officer.
Charles Henry (1794–1878), a son; early naval career, later ordained,
 became rector of Sedgehill, Wiltshire; close friend of his cousin,
 Percy Bysshe Shelley.
For other children, see Fig. 1.

The Pilfolds

Captain John Pilfold (?1776–1834) of Cuckfield, Sussex; surrogate 'father' to his nephew, Percy Bysshe Shelley.

James Pilfold (1771–?) of Effingham, Surrey; a brother of Captain John.

Mrs Shelley (*see above*), a sister.

Mrs Grove (*see above*), a sister.

For Bathia Jackson (*née* Pilfold), a sister, see Fig. 1.

Others

Thomas Medwin (1788–1869), second cousin of the poet and his first biographer.

Thomas Jefferson Hogg (1792–1862), Shelley's Oxford friend and later biographer.

Harriet Westbrook (1795–1816), Shelley's first wife; committed suicide 1816.

Liza Westbrook, her elder sister.

PREFACE

My interest in Shelley's early love affair with his Wiltshire cousin Harriet Grove arose in a quite unpredictable way. The poet who occupied my thoughts at the time was not Shelley but a later admirer of his, Thomas Hardy. A poem of Hardy's entitled 'Concerning Agnes' provoked my curiosity about the identity of his Agnes. When I had established that she was a daughter of General Pitt-Rivers who had married Walter, the son and heir of Sir Thomas Grove of Ferne, I began to search for any papers, letters, diaries, portraits, etc., that might have survived her death in 1926.

I was more amply rewarded than I could have hoped. The Groves were tenacious preservers of documents. Not only did I find Agnes's diaries ranging from 1879 to 1925, with much correspondence besides, but also series of diaries written by her father-in-law Sir Thomas Grove and by Sir Thomas's aunt, Charlotte Grove. Fortified with this wealth of material I was able to publish a full-length biography of Agnes Grove – *Concerning Agnes* – in 1982.

At that point my interest in the Groves should have reached its natural conclusion but I had accumulated so much material about this family, which had lived through at least five centuries within ten miles of my home, that I had a more intimate knowledge of them than of my own ancestors. As I continued to explore the great hoard of papers with growing fascination, I made two startling discoveries. One was in the 1811 diary of Charlotte Grove, the other in a single, unrelated diary for 1810 which remained anonymous.

On a fly-leaf of the 1811 diary Charlotte had written, 'Sorry to hear Bysshe* was expelled Oxford for writing to the Bishops on Atheism'. In the other diary the entries were scanty and often concerned with minor items of expenditure, but as I glanced

* Within his family circle the poet Percy Bysshe Shelley was known by the unusual name he inherited from his grandfather Sir Bysshe Shelley.

through it my attention was caught by the word *Zastrozzi*. I knew just enough of Shelley to recall that this was the title of a piece among his *juvenilia*. I looked at the diary more closely. It was entitled Baxter's Sussex Pocket Book. In a pocket at the back I found a fold of paper enclosing a lock of brown hair coiled round a black seal. The seal bore a cryptic imprint, showing a human eye, a large cross or capital X with peck marks around it, and the words 'a return'. The meaning is plain enough – 'I X-pecked [expect] a return', a corresponding lock of the recipient's hair. On the paper were written the initials H. G., which suggested 'Harriet Grove' to me. I was aware that there had been a romance between Shelley and his cousin Harriet, and that Sussex was Shelley's county.

At this point I turned for help – as I frequently do, and never in vain – to my friend Robert Gittings, who promptly put me in touch with Donald Reiman of the Carl H. Pforzheimer Library in New York. Harriet Grove's diaries for 1809 and 1810 – the years of her close association with Shelley – are preserved in the great collection of Shelley material which is the speciality of the Pforzheimer Library.* The full text of her diaries was published in 1961 as Volume II of *Shelley and his Circle 1773–1822*, a continuing large-scale project of which Dr Reiman is the current editor. With his valuable encouragement I began to scrutinise the traditional version of the Shelley–Harriet Grove romance which had taken shape during the hundred years since Shelley's death, in ignorance of Harriet's diaries and before a forgery of a particularly important Shelley letter had been detected. With the fresh material that I could add it seemed timely to re-examine the whole story and in so doing to give more substance to the rather shadowy background of Shelley's Wiltshire cousins – and his first love, Harriet Grove.

---

* Now located in New York Public Library.

· *Chapter One* ·

In any account of the boyhood and young manhood of the poet Percy Bysshe Shelley, his Wiltshire cousins, the Groves, figure prominently.[1] When he was sent down from Oxford in March 1811, Shelley found refuge in London with his cousin John Grove who lived in Lincoln's Inn Fields and took on the thankless task of trying to mediate with Shelley's irate father. When Shelley needed to get away to a place of solitude and privacy it was his cousin Tom Grove who invited him to stay on the vast Grove estate in Wales at Cwm Elan. When Shelley eloped with Harriet Westbrook the only companion to see him safely aboard the coach to York was Charles Henry Grove, the youngest of the Grove brothers, who many years later wrote down one of the few recollections that have survived of the earlier love affair between Shelley and yet another Grove cousin, Harriet Grove.

It is this romance with Harriet Grove which deeply affected the developing emotional life of Shelley during the years 1809-10, the period of his transition from Etonian schoolboy to Oxford under-graduate and budding author. For the first time he had the experience of falling in love in a more than transient sense. There was an air of genuine commitment, strengthened by the approval of both families. At the beginning of 1809 Shelley was sixteen and a half, Harriet seventeen and a half. Both were therefore entirely dependent on their parents and still largely contained within the unit of the family, though with mounting adolescent impulses to strike out in a personal way. To those of a romantic turn of mind it must have seemed an ideal match, linking the incipient brilliance of the lover with the lively teenage girl who was already becoming an acknowledged beauty. More practical considerations were equally auspicious. As the eldest son, Bysshe Shelley could expect to inherit

1

a newly created baronetcy and a seat in Parliament. Harriet Grove's social background was one of the most respected, wealthy and long-established 'county' families.

The interests of the Shelleys were centred in the vicinity of the town of Horsham in Sussex, and in the patronage of the local grandee, the Duke of Norfolk. Their history was unremarkable until the poet's namesake and grandfather, Bysshe Shelley (1731-1815), amassed a comfortable fortune and rendered political services to the Duke of Norfolk which brought him a baronetcy in 1806.[2]

The Groves emerged in the vicinity of Shaftesbury in the fifteenth century as lawyers serving the Abbess of Shaftesbury and subsequently the Tudor opportunists, Sir Thomas Arundell and the Earl of Pembroke. The manor of Ferne or Fern became their family seat in Wiltshire in the late sixteenth century. Harriet's father, Thomas Grove (1758-1847), was a large landowner, not only in his home territory of Wiltshire and Dorset (see Fig. 2) but in Wales, East Anglia and the Midlands.[3]

What brought the Shelleys of Sussex and the Groves of Wiltshire together was a Horsham family, the White-Pilfolds (see Fig. 1).[4] In addition to their principal seat at Horsham the Whites also owned the manor of Effingham in Surrey. The farming tenant of Effingham, James Pilfold, married a White daughter, Bathia, in about 1760 and their first-born, Elizabeth (1763-1846), married Timothy Shelley and in 1792 became the mother of the poet. Another White daughter married Sir Ferdinand Poole who became Sheriff of Sussex in 1789.[5] According to Tom Medwin, Lady Poole was the aunt who brought up the young Elizabeth Pilfold; she could well have been instrumental in arranging her marriage with Timothy Shelley.

In all, James and Bathia Pilfold had six children. One, Ferdinando, born in 1775, possibly died at an early age. Another, Charles, died in India without issue. James (b. 1771) occupied the property at Effingham and was 'Uncle Jem' to Harriet and Bysshe.[6] The three other Pilfolds each had a close connection with Ferne and its surrounding Wiltshire villages of Donhead St Mary, Donhead St Andrew and Berwick St John. The most obvious is Charlotte (1764-1828), who in 1782 married Thomas Grove and gave birth to five sons and five daughters, including Harriet. Charlotte Grove and her sister Elizabeth Shelley were the main link between the two family territories, but by no means the only one. Their brother John,[7] one of Nelson's captains at Trafalgar, had chosen as a wife a daughter of T. South of Donhead in 1803. Their sister Bathia in 1790 married the Rev. Dr Gilbert Jackson, who was probably related to the rector of Donhead St Mary at that date, Richard Jackson: what is certain is that Gilbert was nominated by Thomas Grove to succeed Richard at Donhead St Mary in 1796.

By 1804, therefore, the kinship of Shelleys and Groves was firmly established through their various Pilfold links. A new generation of children was growing up with an awareness of cousinly relationships. In the spring of 1804 Bysshe Shelley – with his twelfth birthday still to come – visited Ferne and made the acquaintance of the younger Grove children. Of the older ones two – Tom and Emma – were already married; two more – John and William – had left home to start their careers.

At this time Shelley was a pupil at a boarding school, Syon House, at Isleworth on the outskirts of London. His parents had doubtless chosen the school on the recommendation of the Medwins: Thomas Charles Medwin, a Horsham lawyer, was the Duke of Norfolk's steward and the husband of a Pilfold niece of James Pilfold. Their son, Tom Medwin, who became Shelley's first biographer, was already a pupil at Syon House when the decision was taken to send Shelley there – under the protection of his older Medwin cousin.

Two of the Grove boys, Charles Henry and George, were at Harrow School and were to be collected at the end of the winter term in 1804 by one of Mr Grove's servants. A decision was taken to pick up Bysshe Shelley at the same time and bring him back with his two cousins to spend some or all of the school holidays at Ferne. The three were close together in age – Bysshe eleven and a half, George ten and a half, Charles Henry nine and a half. Fortified by his slight seniority, Bysshe's instinctive leadership soon took charge.[8]

The journey to Ferne must have been quite an adventure for Shelley. When Mr Grove drove to and from London he liked to rest overnight halfway. If they made the journey in the day the boys must have been excited but weary after the long final run from Salisbury across the Downs before making the steep descent of Whitesheet Hill to pass the Glove Inn and enter the park of Ferne

House. The house itself, dating back to the fifteenth century, was coming to the end of its effective life: a few years later it had to be evacuated and rebuilt.

Their freshly arrived boy-cousin from distant Sussex would have excited varying degrees of curiosity in the Grove girls, who ranged from the much older Charlotte (twenty-one) to Louisa (eight). His close contemporaries were Harriet and – a year younger – Marianne, who lived only two more years.

What may have passed between Harriet and Bysshe during his visit is not known. The only account of the episode was provided many years later by her brother Charles Henry Grove when Shelley's sister Hellen asked him for his recollections of Shelley in their youth. Writing in 1857, Charles could recount only one incident in the school holiday of 1804:

> Bysshe, who was some few years older than we were, thought it would be good service to play carpenters, and, under his auspices, we got the carpenters' axes, and cut down some of my father's young fir trees in the park. My father often used to remind me of that circumstance. . . .[9]

After the close confinement and severe discipline of Syon House the gleeful abandon in the freedom of the park at Ferne with an axe in one's hand is not difficult to understand; nor of course is Mr Grove's chagrin at the behaviour of his young visitor.

The questions Charles Grove might have answered about those days at Ferne must remain questions. Did Shelley stay for the whole of the school holiday or did he go on to his Sussex home, Field Place? Were any of the Grove children given a reciprocal invitation, perhaps in the summer of the same year, to visit Aunt Shelley? How strong an impression did Shelley and Harriet make on each other at this first meeting? On the later evidence of her diaries, Harriet was a lively and spirited girl who responded with interest to a visitor of her own age.

In September of that year Shelley put Syon House behind him and went to Eton. Charles Grove continued at Harrow until 1805 when he followed the example of his brother William and enlisted in the Royal Navy. By his own testimony, Charles did not see cousin Bysshe again until the spring of 1810 when he went to Field Place with a family party that included Harriet; and he noted that 'Bysshe was at that time more attached to my sister Harriet than I can express.'[10]

Charles's absence from the family circle, until late November 1809 when he wrote from HMS *Bellerophon* to say he was quitting the Navy,[11] deprived him of the opportunity to witness the inception and first flowering of this romantic attachment. It was certainly in train in 1808 and may well have begun earlier. No correspondence between the Groves and Shelleys in the years 1805–8 has survived, nor have any of their diaries or memoirs. The earliest diary of Harriet Grove is for 1809; of her sister Charlotte for 1811; and I have what I am convinced is Shelley's diary for 1810. The only relevant piece of paper with an earlier date is a poem of Shelley's entitled 'To St Irvyne', with the subtitle 'Feb[ry] 28th 1805', included in the collection of early poems that he wrote in a notebook which has come to be known as *The Esdaile Notebook*.[12] The importance of the poem in this present context is that it is a love poem and that at the end of it Shelley wrote 'To H Grove'.

Where nothing is certain, hypothesis flourishes. Could he have written a poem to Harriet in such terms as early as 1805? What can be learnt from the text of the poem itself?

To St Irvyne
Feb[ry] 28th 1805

O'er thy turrets, St Irvyne, the winter winds roar,
    The long grass of thy Towers streams to the blast.
Must I never, St Irvyne, then visit thee more?
    Are those visions of transient happiness past –

When with Harriet I sat on the mouldering height,
    When with Harriet I gazed on the star-spangled sky,
And the August Moon shone thro' the dimness of night?
    How swiftly the moment of pleasure fled by!

How swift is a fleeting smile chased by a sigh!
    This breast, this poor sorrow-torn breast must confess:
Oh Harriet, loved Harriet, tho' thou art not nigh,
    Think not thy lover thinks of thee less.

5

How oft have we roamed thro' the stillness of Eve
 Through St Irvyne's old rooms that so fast fade away.
That these pleasure-winged moments were transient I grieve;
 My Soul like those turrets falls fast to decay.

My Harriet is fled like a fast-fading dream,
 Which fades ere the vision is fixed on the mind,
But has left a firm love and a lasting esteem,
 That my soul to her soul must eternally bind.

When my mouldering bones lie in the cold, chilling grave,
 When my last groans are borne o'er Strood's wide Lea,
And over my Tomb the chill night-tempests rave,
 Then, loved Harriet, bestow one poor thought on me.

To H Grove[13]

In its general tone the poem is adolescent, in pursuit of powerful emotions that the poet would like to feel but is not yet able to do so. It is a conventional pastiche of the tragically devout lover, such as one might find in the juvenilia of many authors. Of closer interest are the facts incorporated in the poem: that in August Harriet had walked in the moonlight with Shelley a number of times at the romantic scene of St Irvyne's – a ruined building near the Shelley home Field Place. She is also presumed to be acquainted with Strood, another local landmark.

When did this happen? The editor of *The Esdaile Notebook*, Kenneth Neill Cameron, whose opinion must carry weight, considers that Shelley was too young to write the poem in 1805 and that Harriet's visit to Field Place took place in August 1808.[14] This implies, however, that Shelley wrote the poem in February 1809 at a time when he and Harriet were frequently exchanging letters – and what must be recognised as mutual love letters. Indeed, on 21 February 1809 Harriet had a letter from Shelley with the good news that she would certainly see him in London, and she commented 'I am so glad of it' – underlining the words to emphasise her pleasure. All through the first quarter of 1809 Harriet's diary indicates a voluminous and happy correspondence. For Shelley to write 'To St Irvyne' at such a time strains credulity to its limit.

If the visit must have been earlier than 1808, how much earlier was it? For lack of any positive evidence for 1807, or 1806, it is tempting to speculate that the poem might after all be factually, literally correct. Shelley's Easter visit to Ferne could reasonably have been followed by a reciprocal invitation for a summer visit by some of the Grove children to Field Place. Harriet, being close in age to the two eldest Shelley children – Bysshe and Elizabeth – would be a likely member of the party. At the age of thirteen, without being unduly precocious, she would be ready to 'try her wings' in the first flights of romance. Growing up with older brothers and sisters in circumstances of class and custom which made the choice of a beau a matter of great moment, it would indeed be odd if Harriet's imagination were not feeling its way towards the exciting private world that lovers create for themselves.

But Shelley – in August 1804? He had just had his twelfth birthday and was about to enter Eton. To be playing the lover in a boy and girl companionship must seem precocious: even so, it is worth examining such evidence as there is. A contemporary of Shelley's at Syon House School, Sir John Rennie, recorded in his autobiography that Shelley 'exhibited considerable poetical talent' when he could not have been more than twelve years old. According to Rennie, 'he used to write verse, English and Latin, with considerable facility'.[15] The benefits of hindsight in Rennie's account must not be disregarded, but Shelley's subsequent career at Eton seems to indicate an early intuitive sense of the poet's destiny.

Emotionally, Shelley had already enjoyed a kind of awakening at Syon House in his 'devoted attachment', as he later recalled it, to 'a boy about my own age'. They poured out their hearts to each other in youthful talk and 'used to speak of the ladies with whom we were in love. . . . Every night, when we parted to go to bed, I remember we kissed each other'.[16] The effect that an attractive and romantically adventurous cousin might have on such a boy is not difficult to predict.

It is also worth recalling that boys of Shelley's class and generation were often required to be precocious in other ways: not for them the sheltered and protracted childhood that many of their grandchildren enjoyed. Harriet's brother William entered the Royal Navy as a first-class volunteer (in effect a gentleman cadet) at the age of ten and saw action against the French a year later. He became a midshipman

three weeks before his fourteenth birthday while serving in the East
Indies, where he spent seven years in all.[17]

Is there any particular significance in the date, 28 February,
attached to the poem? As 'the winter winds roar' in the opening line,
it is a simple and credible explanation that the date refers to the day
of composition. It is not impossible, however, that the date might
have some deeper meaning, enshrining the occasion of their very
first meeting at Ferne in 1804. A later poet, close in sympathy to
Shelley, commemorated a similar event in that way: on Thomas
Hardy's desk were two calendars, one for practical use and the other
permanently arrested at 7 March, the date of Hardy's first meeting
with Emma Lavinia Gifford his future wife.[18] It is an analogy that
will bear only a limited weight, but it is a possibility where so little is
certain. What is not a possibility is the suggestion made by Kenneth
Neill Cameron that Charles Grove's recollection of Shelley's first
visit to Ferne might be mistaken in its year, so that not 1804 but 28
February 1805 was the date when Shelley was collected from school
at Isleworth. Cameron must have overlooked the fact that by 1805
Shelley had left Syon House and was at Eton.[19]

The central fact remains: at some time in the winters of 1805–8
Shelley addressed a love poem to Harriet Grove in which he
presents himself as a lonely figure at home contemplating the
romantic moonlit scenes in which they had walked together during
a previous August. If 1805 is judged to be too soon for Shelley to
have written 'To St Irvyne', 1809 is demonstrably impossible if the
sentiments expressed in the poem are to be believed. During the last
week of February 1809 and the first week of March Harriet's diary
contains entries on seven days which indicate letters received from
Shelley or written by her to him. That hers would have been in
loving terms is beyond doubt. She had not 'fled like a fast-fading
dream'. Quite the contrary. Their correspondence was at its highest
intensity.

In default of firm evidence to the contrary, it is difficult to dismiss
the obvious thought that the date attached by Shelley to the poem
was indeed its date of composition, even though he may have
revised the poem later. If he gave a copy to Harriet Grove it has not
survived and must be regarded as lost in the general obscurity
surrounding Shelley–Grove relationships in the years 1805–8.

Shelley's experiences at Eton are well recorded, but little else. Harriet also may have gone to a boarding school – Miss Willson's at Bath, perhaps, which her younger sister Louisa attended in 1809.[20] In such circumstances correspondence between cousins could easily languish and become fitful, if it were not stimulated by a fresh meeting.

Within the Grove family circle a few events are worth noting, if only to add detail to the general background. In 1805 Harriet's brothers, Charles and George, left Harrow,[21] and their grandmother Grove died. The last of the elders, a widow for thirty-six years, she was buried at Berwick St John.[22]

The following year, 1806, brought a second death, but of a very different and deeply tragic kind. Harriet's fourteen-year-old sister Marianne perished when her muslin dress caught fire and, as she ran for help, she was enveloped in flames.

In the same year the eldest Grove brother, Tom, married Henrietta Farquharson, whose father, generally known as 'Squire' Farquharson, was a celebrated master of foxhounds and a great landowner in Dorset.[23] It was Tom and Henrietta Grove who were to be Shelley's hosts in Wales in 1811 and 1812. The Grove connection with Wales dates back to 1792 when Thomas Grove senior bought the Cwm Elan estate near Rhayader in what then was Radnorshire.[24] Apart from any financial return, the value of Cwm Elan for the Groves was as a summer residence. Later in her life Harriet's sister Charlotte remembered her childhood days when they 'went into Wales'.[25]

A Grove residence of even greater importance to Shelley was the house at 49 Lincoln's Inn Fields which tended to become a London headquarters for both families. The eldest son, Tom Grove, is described as 'of Lincoln's Inn', which suggests that he followed family tradition and chose the law as his profession. The next eldest, John, became a surgeon and was connected in some way with St Bartholomew's Hospital. The house in Lincoln's Inn Fields was certainly John's London base in 1809: a letter of April 1809 from his sister Louisa refers to his housekeeper and footman there. Quite possibly Tom had preceded John as the occupant.[26]

As the younger generation of Shelleys and Groves entered their teens, this London house became valuable as an occasional base and meeting place, and there is no doubt that John Grove saw quite a traffic of visitors from Field Place and from Ferne. The fact that Horsham was less than forty miles from London, as against Ferne's hundred miles, certainly made it easier for the two families to keep in touch – the more so when Shelley was at Eton and his sisters at a school in Clapham. London, then as now, was a magnet for many purposes; the Grove establishment in Lincoln's Inn Fields must have become a familiar and welcome sight to two generations of Groves and Shelleys until at least 1814 when John Grove removed much or all of his furniture to Ferne.[27]

· *Chapter Two* ·

With the dawning of 1809 we are on firmer ground, thanks to the availability of Harriet Grove's diary for that year. The physical history of this and a second diary for the following year are discussed in Appendix One. It is the content of the diary that concerns us immediately.

The period of Christmas and New Year was a time for family gatherings, informal dances and formal balls. Children had returned from their boarding schools and grown-up sons were on vacation from universities or professional occupations. In December 1808, however, Ferne was quieter than usual. At their maximum there would have been ten Grove children in the house in 1803 or 1804. In 1808 there were only three: Harriet, her younger sister Louisa and the much older Charlotte, who was now twenty-six. Of their brothers, William, Charles and George were away at sea. The two eldest, Tom and John, may have paid brief visits over Christmas Day but were absent when Harriet began to write her first entry on the fly-leaf before the diary proper: 'We went to Mr Portman's on Friday and went to a pleasent Ball at Blandford in the Evening came home Saturday 31st of Decr 1808.[1] I have heard that Aunt Shelley gave a Ball on Friday – 30th 1808.'

The remainder of the entry consists of seven words which have been crossed out, but are still legible, and a further passage which has been obliterated. The legible words are 'Bysshe tells me in his letter that' – and the rest is lost. This crossing out of many passages in the diaries appears to be a clumsy or half-hearted attempt to remove all references to Shelley. Where they are still legible I shall quote them without further comment on the extent of the defacement, but the reader should know that somebody – quite

11

possibly Harriet herself – attempted to expunge Shelley from the diaries, and much is indeed totally obliterated.

It was customary for the Groves to stay with their friends the Portmans at Bryanston to attend the Blandford ball at the end of the year. Pleasant as it was, on this occasion Harriet's thoughts must have wandered to that other ball, at Field Place. Given the choice there can be no doubt that she would have preferred Aunt Shelley as her hostess. Instead she returned from Bryanston to Sunday dinner with her other maternal aunt, Bathia Jackson, in company with Aunt Jackson's husband and a curate, Mr Wake, whom Harriet regarded as a bore.

In the first ten days of January Harriet received at least three letters from Shelley and wrote to him once. 'I heard from my dear Bysshe' is how she expresses herself. The words 'my dear' are otherwise reserved exclusively for her immediate family. Clearly their correspondence did not begin in 1809, nor were they strangers to each other. The links between Groves and Shelleys were particularly strong at this time. The Bysshe–Harriet correspondence was not the only one. Louisa Grove and Mary Shelley were writing to each other; so were Harriet and Aunt Shelley. The flow of letters to and from Sussex must have been a notable feature of the mail handled at the Glove Inn, which stood conveniently near the junction of the old coach road from Salisbury as it came down Whitesheet Hill to meet the turnpike road that kept to the lower ground along the Nadder valley. Each day one of the servants from Ferne walked across the park to the Glove, leaving a bag with the outgoing mail and collecting the newly delivered. For Harriet and Louisa, if not for Charlotte, the return of the servant with the mail must have been watched for with discreetly well-mannered expectancy. For teenage girls in their circumstances a letter was a precious signal from a larger world. To emphasise the point, the diary was still new when Harriet was reduced to writing, as the entry for 17 January, 'Nothing particularly happened. Miss Popham did not come'. A letter, even if only from the sisters' friend Letitia Popham, would have made all the difference.

Which members of the two families had met in 1808 is undiscoverable. The convenience of John Grove's residence in Lincoln's Inn Fields as a meeting place has already been indicated and John himself must have been the main link between Field Place and Ferne. He liked to return to his Wiltshire home when he had the opportunity and he eventually settled in Salisbury as physician at the infirmary.[2] He was also a welcome guest with the Shelleys and probably made more visits to Field Place than any of his brothers or sisters. Typically, he was there on 11 January when Harriet wrote to him. The reply she received on the 21st told her he was coming to Ferne with the latest gossip from Field Place. In the following days her diary draws the threads together:

> Jan 22. Sunday. Good gracious a deep snow as Mr Wake is here I am quite afraid he will be snowed in here.[3]
> Jan 23. I hope John will be able to get here tomorrow as I long to see him.
> Jan 24. Dear fellow he is come to our great surprise and pleasure. Heard from dear Bysshe. Mr Wake went away.
> Jan 25. John talked a great deal about the Shelleys he has been spending a week there at that delightful place.

The month ended with a visit to brother Tom and his wife Henrietta at Tarrant Gunville.[4] It was a somewhat disastrous expedition as the carriage overturned on the steep ascent to 'Wind Green'. Win Green, as it is now named, is the highest point in Dorset, 915 feet above sea-level. It rises steeply to the south of Ferne and was a frequent scene of overturning carriages and wagons. The hilltop now belongs to the National Trust, but in Harriet's time it belonged to her father, who eventually had a new road made to reduce the dangers. Fortunately no one was injured on this occasion and Harriet noted that they took no chances on the return journey: 'Walked down Wind Green'.

In February she continued to write to Aunt Shelley. The correspondence with Bysshe was mentioned at least seven times but yields little as the deletions are heavy. Bysshe also wrote to John Grove enclosing a valentine for a Mrs Habbersham. This looks like a Shelleyan prank at the lady's expense, an impression confirmed by an entry in Charlotte Grove's diary on 3 January 1811: 'Heard a most wonderful event, that Mrs Habersham is going to be married'.[5] How Shelley came to think of this lady as a target for a hoax valentine and why John was to be a channel for its delivery are beyond my knowledge, but the fact that Charlotte also knew her reinforces the impression that the cousins shared a great deal of common ground.

Two more February entries are worth mentioning, in passing. One records that 'Dear Dear Louisa is gone back to school.' With no companion now except Charlotte, there is a heartfelt comment, 'I miss her so much'. The other entry reads, 'Took a long walk to Berry Court, the old family mansion. The old woman that lives there is mad'. Lower Berry Court, to give it its modern name, was the ancestral home of the Groves from the fifteenth century onwards until the transfer to Ferne in 1570. The once proud mansion had fallen on hard times, though it has recovered since. Mr Grove, like his friend and neighbour Mr Wyndham at Norrington, had no great reverence for the architecture of the past. Like hermit crabs, these county dynasts moved as they grew into more spacious surroundings and discarded their old shells to be used as quarters for their farm-workers.

A more striking entry is that of 21 February: 'Heard from Bysshe and we shall certainly see him in London. I am so glad of it'. A flurry of letters immediately passed between them, while Harriet also kept up her correspondence with Aunt Shelley. The trip to London was apparently planned by the Groves independently of the Shelleys. A letter from John at the beginning of April said that he 'thinks we shall see Aunt Shelley in Town', but it was therefore uncertain and in fact she did not come. What mattered most to Harriet was that Bysshe was promised. 'I hope this month', she wrote, 'I shall be more fortunate in seeing the person I wish than I was at Christmas.' In thick large letters she added confidently, 'I THINK I SHALL'.

After a day of packing, the Groves set off from Ferne and travelled as far as Halford Bridge, their overnight stopping place. Next day they arrived at Lincoln's Inn Fields, where a long letter from Bysshe was waiting for Harriet. There was another next day, written from Cuckfield where Shelley was staying with Colonel Sergison, of whom there is more to be said later. After a day spent in shopping, Harriet received a third letter from Bysshe which presumably gave her the reassuring news that he was on his way to London. On 16 April she was able to write in her diary: 'Sunday. Dear Bysshe and Mr Shelley arrived here the former I am very glad to see – I think Mr

Shelley appears cross [deletion] for <u>what reason I know not.'</u> Appearing cross was no novelty for Mr Shelley; he did it easily and often. Perhaps he had not expected to meet such a numerous party of his wife's relatives. However, he came to dinner three days later.

In the meantime Harriet had Bysshe's company in sightseeing and theatre-going. There was Miss Fernwood's Exhibition of Worsted to be visited, not to mention the Panorama of Grand Cairo; and *Richard III* was combined with a Dibdin farce, *Mother Goose*. On another day Harriet and Bysshe went to Clapham to visit his sisters Mary and Hellen Shelley at Mrs Fenning's school. In Harriet's opinion her girl cousins were 'the nicest girls I ever saw'. Hellen, who was then nine and a half, recalled many years later the occasion of her brother's visit 'with the elders of the family'. These 'elders' are difficult to identify but there is a precise reference to 'Harriet Grove, his early love' who was one of the party. 'How fresh and pretty she looked!' is Hellen's comment, adding, 'Her assistance was invoked to keep the wild boy quiet, for he was full of pranks, and upset the port-wine on the tray cloth, for our school-mistress was hospitable and had offered refreshments'. When they went into the garden, where Bysshe could cause less chaos, 'there was much ado to calm the spirits of the wild boy'.[6]

In all the two lovers had four days together before it was time for Bysshe to depart. Harriet immediately wrote him 'a good letter' and he sent her some songs which they must have been talking about, as she refers to them as 'the songs'.* Before he left London he chose a pink dress as a gift for Charlotte and Harriet. Presumably a social nicety forbade such a gift to Harriet only, though there was no doubting the intention. Charlotte presented it to her young sister, who commented rather primly, 'I am very much obliged to them'.

The Groves stayed on in London for four more weeks. During this period Harriet wrote three letters to Aunt Shelley and received four from her. The evident *rapport* between them is a striking feature in the whole Shelley–Grove relationship. Harriet also had a letter from Mary Shelley, following the visit to the Clapham school.

---

* In their usage, 'songs' could mean poems.

15

Bysshe's letters continued, with an 'immense long' one on 29 April. Harriet makes no mention of any that she sent to him, perhaps because her diary is filled with the many events of these London days. She went to operas and plays, rode in Hyde Park, went with Lady Fraser to a rout at Lady Glyn's, heard an excellent sermon at the Foundling Chapel, went to the Tower, St Paul's and Westminster Abbey, and attended dinner parties at which members of the family appeared – the Longs and Rudges on her father's side;[7] John Waddington, who in 1805 had married Harriet's eldest sister Emma; and Mr Shelley with Colonel Sergison. Some of their Wiltshire neighbours were also in town for the season and giving or attending dinner parties – the Knellers of Donhead Hall, the Stills of East Knoyle and Annabella Cooke of Donhead Lodge, widow of the gallant captain of *Bellerophon* who had been killed at Trafalgar.

Reading between the lines, it seems that the Grove parents planned this London excursion for more than its obvious social pleasures. There were the opportunities to entertain friends and relatives, and thus to maintain contact with them. If Mr Grove bore the main expense of 49 Lincoln's Inn Fields,* as is probable, the opportunity for an annual visit in the spring would justify it, particularly with growing and marriageable daughters.

An increasingly acute problem was Charlotte's single state at twenty-six. Her parents doubtless wished to see her 'settled', and she was certainly not unwilling. One of Harriet's entries during the London visit in 1809 reads, 'The Stills dined here rather a stupid party Charlotte flirted as usual with W. Long'. When they returned to Ferne in late May, the Groves brought Walter Long with them. Charlotte and Harriet took sociable walks with him but Harriet wearied of his 'nonsensical conversation'. No more was heard of him until October when they learned he was going to marry Lady Mary Carnegie.[8] Another potential beau for Charlotte had been intro-

* It may be no coincidence that William Long also had a house in Lincoln's Inn Fields, so the Grove presence there may stem from the earlier alliance of Mr Grove's father with the Longs. William Long, a surgeon at St Bartholomew's Hospital for thirty-three years, became Master of the Royal College of Surgeons, which is situated in Lincoln's Inn Fields.

duced in London by Mr Shelley: this was Colonel Sergison, who came into some prominence in her life a year later. Meanwhile the one immediate result of the London visit was that Harriet and Bysshe had added new depth and substance to their relationship by the four days spent in each other's company. To be closely together when for so long their love had to subsist on a diet of letters was a rare delight; and to be seen together publicly as recognised lovers was a pleasure that adolescents particularly relish. Writing to a fellow Etonian[9] on 7 April, Shelley said, 'I shall be in London on the 16th at the Opera on Tuesday – observe who I am with & I will ask your opinion at some future period'. Understandably, he wanted Harriet to be noticed and himself envied. The 16th was indeed the date when he arrived at 49 Lincoln's Inn Fields, and it is interesting that he knew well in advance of the plans that had been made, though he made a mistake in the day. It was on the Wednesday, not the Tuesday, that Shelley accompanied Harriet and the family party to a comic opera by Dibdin, *The Cabinet*.[10] Mr Shelley was perhaps their host for the occasion.

The Groves arrived back at Ferne on 21 May, and at once there is a change in Harriet's diary. The correspondence with Aunt Shelley continues, but Harriet is much less engaged in writing and reading letters. It is as if the social excitement of London and the days with Bysshe have at least partially satisfied her hunger for correspondence. She scarcely mentions her absent brothers. In the course of four weeks Bysshe's name appears twice and there are half a dozen deletions which may be presumed to refer to him. One good reason for any decline in her general interest in the comings and goings of the mail coach may be that she had scarcely returned from London before she was plunged into another whirl of social festivities at Salisbury, where, she said, 'We are so gay here more so than in Town'. At the end of it all she had a long rest on a Sunday morning, not rising until 10 a.m., 'to recruit after all this raking'.

She was then preoccupied with other matters. An ominous crack developed in the front wall of Ferne House and it quickly became obvious that the building would have to be evacuated, demolished and rebuilt. On her eighteenth birthday, 26 June 1809, Harriet recorded: 'Such a bustle left dear old Fern Mama and Louisa went in the pheaton [*sic*] with two family pictures before them and

Charlotte and myself walked to the parsonage Lower Donhead* and very very busy unpacking.'[11]

They were soon settled and in early July the postal traffic was back to a high level. Between the 6th and the 11th Harriet received letters from Bysshe and replied to them three times, which means that they were maintaining a correspondence by daily return of post. Next day Harriet's mother heard from Aunt Shelley that Elizabeth Shelley had invited John Grove to Field Place; and on the day after Harriet had letters from Aunt Shelley and from Bysshe. In the three following days, 14–16 July, Louisa heard from Mary Shelley, Harriet had at least two letters from Bysshe – reference to a probable third being obliterated – and wrote to him once. The exchange of signals between Field Place and Donhead St Andrew rectory was becoming almost a cottage industry; and when Harriet went visiting, for example to her married sister Emma at Little Park in Hampshire,[12] she made sure that Bysshe knew the address in advance: when she arrived a letter from him was awaiting her.

At the end of July her brother John was staying at Field Place and Harriet began to believe that she too had a chance of going there during the summer. 'It makes me very happy', she commented. On the first day of August she wrote in her diary, 'What a pleasant month this was last year' – a strangely inconsequential remark which must suggest the possibility that she had visited Field Place then. If so, she was unlikely to be so fortunate in the present year, as a letter from Elizabeth Shelley made her 'afraid Mr Shelley won't ask us to Field Place this summer'. A few days later she walked with her mother and talked to her 'upon a subject that always interests me'. The enigmatic phrasing hardly disguises what the subject would be.

So the summer of 1809 passed, with Bysshe and Harriet maintaining their correspondence but having no opportunity to meet again since their April days in London. The opposite was the case with John Grove and Elizabeth Shelley, between whom there was a growing friendship, with John being a welcome visitor to Field Place. All four would have been in each other's confidence and Elizabeth now began writing to Harriet. On 29 August Harriet noted,

* Donhead St Andrew rectory, latterly known as Donhead House.

'Elizabeth has sent me my picture' – a particularly interesting and ambiguous statement. Should the words 'my picture' be understood as 'a picture of me', a portrait? If so, it could be the unsigned pencil portrait of Harriet at this age, which is the only representation of her that is known to have survived. Elizabeth Shelley was an amateur artist of more than ordinary accomplishment. Tom Medwin said of her that she 'possessed a talent for oil-painting that few artists have acquired'.[13] When Charlotte Grove visited Field Place in 1833 she wrote, 'Elizabeth's oil paintings are very beautiful: the dining and drawing rooms furnished with them'.[14]

The unanswerable question is, when had Harriet and Elizabeth been in each other's company? August 1808 at Field Place may be inferred from the scanty evidence. Elizabeth did not come to London in April 1809 with her father and Bysshe, and neither girl wrote to the other until August. As Elizabeth was the oldest of Shelley's sisters she would be Harriet's obvious feminine counterpart, but her attention was probably concentrated on John Grove as Bysshe's was on Harriet. However, September brought a noticeable change. On 5 September Harriet not only received a letter from Bysshe but also 'got a quiz from Elizabeth'. On the 19th Elizabeth wrote her 'a most affectionate letter', to which Harriet replied next day; and a week later Elizabeth wrote again. They were now embarked on a more or less regular correspondence, while at the same time the exchange of letters with Bysshe either ceased temporarily or was not recorded. Knowing how intensely Elizabeth was dominated by Bysshe at this time as his lieutenant, it must be a possibility that Elizabeth was being used, for some fresh reason, as his channel of communication with Harriet. Significantly, on 13 October Harriet 'heard from ES. She has sent me some verses of Bysshe's – which I think very good' (a sentiment later crossed out incompletely).

The virtual disappearance of Shelley from Harriet's diary in the last quarter of 1809 has prompted some of Shelley's biographers to find an explanation by bringing forward the events of the summer of 1810 as they were later described by Charles Grove. In his letter to Hellen Shelley in 1857, Charles wrote that Harriet 'became uneasy at the tone of his [Shelley's] letters on speculative subjects, at first consulting my mother, and subsequently my father also on the subject'.[15] The publication of Harriet's diaries should have put an end to the suggestion that Charles made a mistake in the date, since it was shown that he did not leave the Navy and return home until the end of 1809. The events he describes belong indubitably to 1810. Of the impassioned letter-writing of 1809 Charles knew no more than he might have gleaned from the occasional letters from home that reached him on his naval voyages.

The behaviour of the parents, on both sides, remains inscrutable throughout. Harriet rarely mentions her parents, unlike her sister Charlotte who had a great affection for her father, referring to him teasingly as 'the little man' and remarking fondly how much he was missed whenever he was away from home, even for a single night. It may be that, with such a numerous family, Mr Grove became more remote from the younger children, as did their mother also in a lesser degree. Whatever the reason, Harriet's diaries offer the minimum of clues to her parents' attitudes towards her. Charles later asserted that there existed an engagement between his sister and Bysshe which had the approval of both fathers.[16] Just when the approval was given and when it began to waver are matters for conjecture.

The temporary lodging of the Groves, during the rebuilding of Ferne, at Donhead St Andrew rectory, was destined to be brief. The rector, who had no need of the building for his own use, died in August and, as his successor wished to occupy the rectory, the Groves searched for alternative accommodation, which they found in Tollard Royal. Again it seems probable that an unoccupied rectory was the answer. The most suitable house in the village would have been King John's House, as it is still named, but it can be ruled out since Harriet went out walking with her friend Helen Tregonwell on 18 November at Tollard and 'shewed King John's House to Helen'.

The rector of Tollard Royal at this time was John Helyar, who, in addition to the rectory, certainly owned a house in Tollard Farnham* and evidently chose to live there with his wife while the Groves were at Tollard Royal.[17] Harriet speaks specifically of going to Farnham to call on him. Her diary contains several references to

---

* The two villages are contiguous, though Tollard Royal is in Wiltshire and Tollard Farnham in Dorset.

the excellence of his sermons and he and his wife were soon on friendly terms with the Groves.

As the Helyars were to play so important a part in Harriet's life, they merit a fuller description here.[18] The Rev. John was a younger brother of William Helyar of Coker Court, near Yeovil, which had been the family seat since 1616. The list of sheriffs of the county of Somerset includes Helyars in 1661, 1701, 1764 and 1768; in 1829 the name of William Helyar junior was added. In addition to the estate of East Coker, William Helyar senior held land at Sedgehill in what had also long been Grove country (Sedgehill is only about five miles north-west of Ferne). The heads of the two families therefore were acquainted with each other and shared common interests. They had jointly pursued a legal action against the ecclesiastical authorities in Sedgehill in 1796, relating to the farmland they owned in the parish.

In 1798 Mr Helyar built a substantial house in Sedgehill beside the road from Shaftesbury to East Knoyle. This was a potential dower house – should he predecease his wife, as he in fact did – and meanwhile it became the establishment of his eldest son and heir, William junior. Harriet's first acquaintance with the Helyars, therefore, was as friends of her father's who had unexpectedly come into prominence as a result of the demolition of Ferne. She had some difficulty at first in spelling their name correctly.

In the midst of the disturbance of moving from Donhead St Andrew to Tollard Royal there was a moment of unexpected pleasure which must be recorded here in Harriet's own words: 'Joy Joy Joy William dear dear William's come home'. Next day she wrote a great many letters 'to tell the joyful event'. Her brother had been away from home, serving in the East Indies for nearly seven years.[19] Now a young man of nineteen he was, in Harriet's eyes, so altered that she felt she would not have recognised him. In the next few weeks he went hunting with his father, travelled to his married sister Emma's house at Little Park and went to visit the Shelleys at Field Place. Harriet records these details of family life in a relaxed and equable manner, with no envy of the ease with which her brothers go to Field Place while she is unable to do so. She was evidently not cherishing any hope of an invitation to spend Christmas there this year.

All too soon William had to join HMS *Orestes* for a short cruise. No

sooner had he departed than fresh naval intelligence of a very different sort arrived. Brother Charles had sailed into Yarmouth on board the *Bellerophon*, still disliking naval life as a profession, and wrote to declare his intention to leave the service and come home. On his way he probably spent some time in London with his brother John, discussing with him the choice of another, more congenial profession. On his arrival at Ferne on 17 December Charles announced his plan to emulate John and become a physician. 'We all like it very much', Harriet commented, recording on the following day, 'Charles began studying Greek. We are a very happy party'.

The year ended in that close family mood, though with Elizabeth Shelley maintaining the correspondence with Harriet, writing letters that Harriet described as 'very drole' (a favourite word of hers). Over Christmas her brother Tom was in a very droll humour and made them all laugh. A second Shelley letter-writer was Mary, who continued to write to Louisa. These two schoolgirls seem to have struck up a continuing friendship and naturally exchanged gossip about their elders. In her latest letter, on 21 December, Mary Shelley told Louisa of a rumour that Harriet was going to be married. Harriet refrained from comment in her diary, limiting her entry to the not very enlightening words, 'Put beads upon our gowns'. The restraint of her diary entries in such contexts is a personal characteristic that must always be borne in mind.

• *Chapter Three* •

Mary Shelley 'has heard that I am going to be married'. How had she heard and what gave rise to such a rumour? Had she been prompted by Bysshe or Elizabeth to fish for information? Had any of Harriet's elder brothers or sisters made some indiscreet remark at Field Place or in a letter? There is no positive answer, but it is worth examining the available evidence so far as the finger points to William Helyar as the subject of the rumour.

It was at the beginning of September that Harriet first mentioned the Helyars in her diary. On the 5th she went to Tollard Royal to inspect the house – in my view it was John Helyar's rectory – to which the family was expecting to move. 'We all like it pretty well', she wrote, adding next day, 'John dines at Mr W. Hilyar's today'. It is reasonable to assume that her brother John already had some acquaintance with young Helyar from encounters in the hunting field. The Groves were a keen hunting family. Mr Grove had his own pack of foxhounds and also ran harriers and beagles. When William Helyar was in residence at Sedgehill he would naturally hunt with the Groves in the accepted neighbourly way.

Having entertained John Grove to dinner, Helyar responded to an invitation to join a dinner party a few days afterwards at the Groves'. A month later he called briefly. A further six weeks elapsed before he reappeared at a Grove dinner party at which his uncle, the Rev. John, was also a guest, accompanied by his wife. A week later it was the John Helyars who entertained the same party to dinner.

At the beginning of December it was hunting that brought William Helyar into closer intimacy with the Groves. He dined with them on the 1st and joined in a pleasant little dance afterwards. Next day he returned with Mr Grove after a day's hunting with the hounds of a celebrated hunting parson, the Rev. William Chafin of

Chettle. On the 3rd, in readiness for further hunting, he came to the Groves after his Uncle John's Sunday church service and the following morning 'breakfasted here', as Harriet recorded, 'and went hunting with my father who had a very pretty run at first close to the house. They went afterwards to Fern'.

That was the last Harriet saw of William Helyar before the rumour of her impending marriage came from Mary Shelley on 21 December. Apart from the pleasant little dance after a family dinner party, there had been very little opportunity to develop their casual acquaintance. Helyar seems at this stage to have been more interested in hunting than in Harriet. Nevertheless, he was an extremely eligible bachelor of about the right age for Harriet – thirty-one to her eighteen. That thought might have occurred to John Grove and would certainly have done so to Charlotte, who was an inveterate matchmaker in a romantic vein where her brothers and sisters were concerned. In passing on the latest gossip from Wiltshire, the move from Donhead to Tollard Royal and the consequent strengthening of a neighbourly bond with the Helyars would be the obvious titbits. What was perhaps no more than the proverbial nod and a wink may have been interpreted more weightily than the circumstances justified.

Oddly, it was on the day after Mary Shelley's letter arrived that Harriet first revealed an interest in William Helyar. On 22 December her diary reads, 'Went to the Shaftesbury ball. Had a most excellent Ball more than 20 Couple. Danced thro' two with Mr Wm H'. On the 28th she records flatly, 'Mr W Helyar came here', and the reason for his presence seems to be adequately and unexcitingly accounted for by the next day's entry: 'Got up early as the Gentlemen went out hunting'. She did not see him again for three months. Any suggestion that in December 1809 Harriet broke off her relationship with Shelley in favour of William Helyar does not bear examination.

Before leaving 1809 there is an incident worth considering for the light it throws on Shelley's conduct as a letter-writer. Mrs Felicia Hemans, who published her first book of poems at a very tender age, recalled later in her life the 'extraordinary' letters from Shelley 'with which I was once persecuted'. This episode was recorded by Tom Medwin[1] and can be placed in the period 1808–9. In 1808 he subscribed to a volume of poems by Felicia Dorothea Browne (Mrs Hemans's maiden name), published in Liverpool when the young author was in her fifteenth year. Medwin ordered the book on the strength of meeting Felicia when she visited his hosts in North Wales. He was impressed by her poems and frequently discussed them with Shelley, who was enthusiastic in his admiration of them and 'with a prophetic spirit he foresaw the coming greatness of that genius, which under the name of Hemans afterwards electrified the world'.

What followed is best told in Medwin's words:

> He desired to become acquainted with the young authoress, and using my name wrote to her, as he was in the habit of doing to all those who in any way excited his sympathies. This letter produced an answer, and a correspondence of some length passed between them, which of course I never saw, but it is supposed that it turned on other subjects besides poetry. I mean, that it was sceptical.

Sceptical of conventional attitudes to religion and marriage it very probably was, and to an inflammatory degree. So much so that Felicia's mother wrote to Tom Medwin's father begging him to use his influence with Shelley to stop any further correspondence. And there the account of the episode ends, at the very point where one wants to know more. Did Shelley's father come to hear of it and perhaps take some action? Did Harriet's father? To stop Shelley from writing letters, particularly when he was not under the parental roof but at Eton, would be a formidable task. Harriet would have been more biddable if her father exerted any pressure on her, but there is no evidence that he did so. What does emerge, however, is that she could receive a letter from Shelley without recording it in her diary. It is unwise to assume that her diaries provide a comprehensive inventory of all letters received from Shelley or written to him. As I have already suggested, the sudden emergence of Elizabeth Shelley as a channel of communication is sufficient ground for the suspicion that the diaries are sometimes more opaque than transparent.

The 1810 diary is positively defective at the outset. The page for the first six days of January has been torn out. The explanation could be a trivial one, but it gains significance from the mutilation of the last entry page in the previous year, where 31 December is wholly removed and the 30th partially so. This is the time of year when some reference to Field Place might be expected. The context implies a recent letter from Elizabeth or Bysshe, as on the 7th Harriet has just received some gossip about Colonel Sergison which she imparts to Charlotte, to the effect that the Colonel is contemplating making a proposal of marriage to a Miss Carter of Horsham – a rumour later dispelled by Elizabeth. During the twenty-five undamaged entries in January, Harriet received two letters from Elizabeth and wrote to her twice. She also had two letters from Aunt Shelley. In addition, she heard on the 9th from her brother John, 'who has been at Field Place and been very gay there and liked his visit very much'. When she next heard from him, three weeks later, Mr Shelley and Bysshe had dined with him at Lincoln's Inn Fields. There is no hint of anything amiss.

Life at home in Tollard Royal continued agreeably. Charlotte and Harriet went to a ball at Blandford as the guests of the Portmans, staying at Bryanston overnight. Next day Mrs Portman sent them as far as Thorny Down in her chaise and four. The inn at Thorny Down on the Great Western Turnpike was a suitable meeting-place for the Grove barouche to take them up and convey them to the Cranborne home of their friends the Tregonwells. Lewis-Dimoke-Grosvenor Tregonwell was the farsighted landowner who founded the town of Bournemouth. He sometimes took the Grove children to his villa on what was then an almost deserted coast. His daughter Helen was an exact contemporary and intimate friend of Charlotte Grove.

Harriet's critical appraisal of young men is well shown in her entry on 21 January: 'Mr Napper Tregonwell preached here he dined with us with a friend of his a Mr Skinner they are neither very Gentlemanlike'. Her 'Napper Tregonwell' was correctly the Rev. John Tregonwell Napier,[2] aged twenty-five and in love with Mr Skinner's sister. He was also a mad keen hunter, for which reason William Chafin made him rector of Chettle. The Prince of Wales, who kept a pack of hounds in Cranborne Chase at this time, spoke of Napier as 'my little foxhunting friend'.

Napier had preached at Tollard to deputise for John Helyar, who had other matters on his mind. He denied rumours that he was intending to move permanently to Bath, but local speculation was well founded though it was not until May that he and his wife departed.

A cryptic reference to some verses received anonymously by Charlotte seems to hint at a prank in the Shelleyan mode and is perhaps to be associated with the false rumour about Colonel Sergison, but nothing further transpired immediately.

The diary for February 1810 is interesting in one or two unusual features. Probably because of the weather, there is more emphasis on the detail of home-life. The month began with days of incessant rain, followed by a prolonged period of deep snow. 'Went a most dirty walk' and 'so wet we none of us stirred out' are typical comments. Harriet enjoyed Louisa's companionship: they liked to sit together in the drawing room with their sketching materials and preserve a mood of intimacy. When Mrs John Helyar rang the doorbell they grabbed their handiwork and ran upstairs. At night they shared a room, where Charles joined them in the evening for conversation, no doubt by turns earnest and lighthearted, while the rest of the family was downstairs. Sadly, the time came for Louisa to return to her boarding school at Bath and a miserable Harriet wrote, 'Quite stupified by staying indoors miss dear Louisa more than ever'. To make matters worse Aunt Philippa Grove, who always talked incessantly, arrived just before the snow fell and drifted to a depth that imprisoned her for eight days before there was a thaw. Tempers became a little shorter than normal. Aunt Grove gave Charles 'a sort of a lecture'. Harriet too became critical of Charles. When it was too wet for him to go out 'he came annoying us', and when they were able to take a long walk together Harriet reflected afterwards, 'I do not quite like his sentiments he thinks too much of appearances'.

During the month Harriet had two letters from Elizabeth Shelley and replied to both. The severe weather must have made difficulties for the mail coaches, but there is a general feeling of withdrawal into the home circle and a reduced interest in Field Place. It is only the second month in which Harriet makes no mention of Aunt Shelley. The one really striking letter comes not from Sussex but from brother William. Cruising in the *Orestes*, he took part in the recapture of a small vessel from the French, but in the meantime he found an opportunity to send a letter to Charlotte, saying of Harriet, 'he thinks I shall never be married that I do not care whether I ever do or not. He says he thinks I never liked any one so much as [deleted] that is a thing no one will <u>ever</u> know but myself'.

Coming from William this is unexpected and difficult to interpret. Less than five months had passed since his return after an absence of seven years. During that absence he would have had occasional letters from home giving him the family gossip, but such emphatic views as he now expressed seem more intuitive than well grounded. He evidently touched a tender spot, if one may judge from Harriet's passionate response. The name that William mentioned as her true love remains Harriet's secret, as she vowed it would. It is tempting to read the name 'Bysshe' into the deletion, and yet there is a 'pastness' in the tone of William's comment which seems to look a little further back. And did she care whether she married or not? That was not a clinching decision which she had to make while her nineteenth birthday lay ahead of her.

On the last day of February William returned for a few happy days with Harriet before he departed to Plymouth to join HMS *Scipion*. They walked together to Rushmore Lodge, the summer residence and hunting headquarters of George Pitt, the second Baron Rivers and Lord of Cranborne Chase;* they played 'Commerce' in the evenings when Willy made them all laugh by his great earnestness; and, in true naval fashion, he gave Charles a haircut. And then he was gone – 'I hope only for a short time', Harriet added. He was the nearest to her in age, less than a year and a half older; despite his long absence, 'dear good-tempered Willy' clearly had a special place in her affections.

Just before he left, a parcel arrived which stirred Harriet's affections in another way and more urgently. She expressed herself as 'most agreeably surprised' by the parcel and the letter that accompanied it 'from my greatest friend'. Whatever words she wrote after that have been deleted. If there could be any doubt that the sender was Shelley it must be dispelled by the entry in *his* diary

---

* The lordship carried the valuable franchise to the exclusive preservation of deer throughout the Chase – an increasingly controversial and contested privilege at this time.

for 1 March: 'Parcel to Harriet';[3] the receipt of the parcel was noted by Harriet four days later. She wrote immediately to Elizabeth Shelley, not to Bysshe overtly. Neither his name nor the contents of the parcel are mentioned until three days later when a long entry has over twelve lines cancelled. All that can be deciphered is 'Shewed the poem [deletion] They [deletion] think it nonsense [deletion]'.

To whom the poem was shown is not specified. Within the family circle at that precise time were Harriet's sister Charlotte, her brother Charles and their friend Helen Tregonwell, in addition to Harriet's parents. If the words 'think it nonsense' reflect their response to the poem it is probable that Charles was the harshest critic. The general impression of him is of a restlessly discontented and rather bumptious sixteen-year-old who would be ready to disparage.

Two days later Harriet 'sent B . . . poem away', which presumably means she had been asked to return it with her comments. Her rumoured collaboration[4] with Shelley in some of his writing at this time may have taken the form of responsive comments and suggestions. She was sufficiently well read to be as much in harmony with Shelley's preoccupation with the Gothic horror vogue as her equivalent today would be with science fiction.

After a comparative lull in Grove–Shelley correspondence during February, there is now a sudden awakening of activity, almost as if those involved were emerging from hibernation. During March Harriet's diary includes four references to her correspondence with Elizabeth, five references to Bysshe and four to Field Place. It becomes clear that Mr Grove is planning an April visit to London, similar to the previous year's. *En route* to London he might wish to make a detour to Little Park to see his newly born grandson, in which case it would be reasonable to call in at Field Place afterwards and spend a day or two there before the final stage to Lincoln's Inn Fields. It is on those lines that Harriet's thoughts were running, as they did with the approach of each of Bysshe's vacations from Eton. A constant feature of her diaries is the longing for an invitation to Field Place at the times – Easter, August and Christmas – when her 'dear Bysshe' would be there.

So it was in March 1810. 'I have sent Elizabeth Shelley a letter', she noted, 'which I hope may be the means of our going to dear Field

Place on our way to Town'. Just how she could influence such a decision is difficult to imagine, but she evidently realised that there was an obstacle. Her enjoyable correspondence with Aunt Shelley seems to have faltered at the end of January and her own mother was showing an unexpected reluctance to include Field Place in the itinerary. Once again Harriet faced the prospect of a last-minute disappointment. Even when the Shelleys wrote to say 'they shall be most happy to see us', Mrs Grove's unwillingness persisted. In despair Harriet wrote, 'I fear owing to some fancy my mother has in her head we shall not go for which I feel the greatest sorrow as I had made up my mind for the pleasure of spending a few days at dear Field Place'. The nature of Mrs Grove's fancy is not revealed; for whatever reason, she appears to have believed that they would not be welcome, despite the assurance given.

When she finally relented she did so grudgingly. In an entry of 27 March that begins with a deletion, Harriet recorded with obvious relief, 'At last they say they will go to Field Place for one day'. For such a visit it was uncommonly, almost pointedly, brief; but it was indeed better than nothing. Harriet wrote at once to Elizabeth to announce the good news, adding, 'It makes me so happy'. Nearly a year had passed since she last saw Shelley. Her eagerness for a reunion is understandable and touching.

The following day brought another welcome surprise. A package arrived, addressed to Harriet and also – perhaps tactfully – to Charlotte. It contained a copy of *Zastrozzi*, a work of transpontine fiction by Shelley, calculated to make even 'Monk' Lewis look tame. Publication had apparently been delayed by several months, as Shelley's diary has the following entry for 15 January: '30 copies of Zastrozzi to come – not to forget Harriet'. After 'Harriet' is what may be an ampersand and a brief deletion followed by two crosses. The significance of the two crosses is not apparent: they could conceivably be kiss symbols. A further entry on 18 February records a similar expectation: 'Zastrozzi to come out 30 copies'.[5] Publication was eventually listed in April, with a few advance copies reaching Shelley at Eton at the end of March. The manner of Harriet's entry in her diary implies that she was already familiar with the existence of the book and of a delay in its publication: 'Bysshe has sent C and me Zastrozzi as it is come out'. There is even the suggestion that she collaborated in some measure in its composition.[6] Tom Medwin claimed explicitly to have been told by Shelley that some of the chapters 'were by Miss Grove'. If so, she must have been disappointed and irritated by her brother's reaction: 'Charles does nothing but abuse Bysshe's romance. I believe he does it the more because he thinks it makes him appear a great man, but I think it makes him appear very illnatured to criticise it so <u>very</u> much'.

However, it was time now for the final preparations for the family's spring tour to sister Emma at Little Park, to brother John in London and – best of all, if only briefly – to 'dear Field Place'. There were even to be one or two lesser stops on the way, so much thought had to be given to the difficult question of what to pack and what to omit. No wonder Harriet wrote sadly, 'They have given Charlotte and me such a little bit of a trunk'.

Leaving Tollard Royal on 2 April they made a brief stop at Compton Chamberlayne, the home of the Penruddockes. On this occasion Mrs Penruddocke, described by Harriet as 'more romantic than ever', did not talk quite so much about Napoleon. From Compton it was a short drive to Aunt Philippa Grove at Nether-hampton, near Salisbury. While they were there Harriet and Charlotte entertained themselves by reading a 'Monk' Lewis novel.

Their next stop was at Southampton where their host was Mr Bromley, who normally lived at Bishopstone, one of the Chalke valley villages between Salisbury and Tollard Royal, where he was a rural dean with some influence in maritime affairs, due presumably to his wife's being a sister of an admiral. They all took a stroll on the quay at Southampton before making their next call, at Little Park. Here the centre of attention was sister Emma's newest baby, George Grove Waddington, named in honour of his uncle who was then in China.

A surprising addition to the family party here was another of the baby's seafaring uncles, William, whose ship had probably put into Portsmouth for a brief shore-leave. At first Harriet feared he would not be able to go on to Field Place with them, but on 14 April 'Dear William says he shall go to Field Place with us which I am glad of. How happy I feel at the idea of going there'.

The baggage was put back in the Grove barouche, the four horses began to pull, and the party set off into Sussex and towards Horsham. Throughout 1809 Harriet's hopes of visiting Field Place had been repeatedly dashed. At last she could count the final hours before she must arrive there.

· *Chapter Four* ·

The distance from Little Park to Field Place, by crow-flight, is about forty miles. By a barouche in 1810, with pauses for refreshment, it probably took the best part of the day to cover the distance of at least fifty miles by road. The Groves spent two nights at Field Place before moving on to Mrs Grove's brother, Captain John Pilfold, at Cuckfield. At the best, therefore, Harriet would have enjoyed Shelley's company during the evening of her arrival, throughout the whole of the next day, and in the following morning. The events of that brief time have been so variously interpreted that it is advisable to recall what Harriet herself wrote in her diary.

April 16. Left L P very early got to dear F P [deletion] they are all very glad to see us. I can not tell what to make of it very strange.

April 17. Still more odd. Walked to Horsham saw the old house St Irvyne had a long conversation but more perplexed than ever walked in the evening to Strood by moonlight.

April 18. This morning we went – before we left the pleasantest party in the world for the most unpleasant – to Horsham, that is E, B & my brothers & self. I still know not what is meant We reached Cuckfield to dinner. What a disagreeable place after the one we have just left.

April 19. Walked in Col. S[ergison's] park very pretty I daresay but my thoughts won't let me think about it.

First, to clarify the locations: 'St Irvyne' was Hill Place, a property belonging to Lady Irwin or Irwine that the Duke of Norfolk was in the process of acquiring. It lay south-east of Field Place: the ruined house was said to have been Elizabethan, the grounds laid out by Capability Brown. Strood, the property of John Commerell, lay in the opposite direction, north-west of Field Place. Colonel Sergison's estate was Cuckfield Place, which he had inherited in 1806, two years after the death of his wife.

What dominates Harriet's account, and must surprise the reader, is her persisting mood of unresolved perplexity. The deletion on the 16th presumably gave a first impression of Shelley's greeting when she arrived. The reception she was given by the Shelleys in general, and Bysshe in particular, is evidently pleasing to her: 'all very glad to see us' and 'the pleasantest party in the world' leave no doubt on that score. To emphasise the point still further it is worth recalling Charles Grove's note of the occasion.[1] Having left the Royal Navy only four months previously, he was now meeting Bysshe again for the first time in six years; and what struck him was that, in his own words, 'Bysshe was at that time more attached to my sister Harriet than I can express'. To account for Harriet's bewilderment by asserting groundlessly, as a recent biographer has done,* that Shelley 'was sulking' requires a perverse genius for flying in the face of the evidence. If any inference can safely be drawn it must be that Mrs Grove's 'fancy' had caused her, from whatever motive, to give Harriet a seriously misleading idea of what to expect when they arrived at Field Place. Throughout the whole affair the policies and interventions of the parents, on both sides, are cloaked in obscurity but must have been influential.

A legend has been fostered that it was on this occasion that Bysshe and Harriet enjoyed a number of moonlit walks and twilit rambles to St Irvyne's and Strood, in a romantic foursome with Elizabeth Shelley and Charles Grove. This springs from Charles's rose-tinted memories in his latter years, when the poem 'To St Irvyne' perhaps became fused with the events of 1810. Harriet's diary makes it clear that there was one moonlit walk, to Strood. Earlier that day they had walked to Horsham, seeing 'the old house St Irvyne' on their way. There was a second visit to Horsham the following morning, when for the first time Harriet refers to the members of the party – Elizabeth, Bysshe, her brothers Charles and William, and herself. The omission of Charlotte, an enthusiastic walker, may be an oversight.

* Richard Holmes, *Shelley: the Pursuit* (London, 1974), p. 19.

For Harriet the sight of Strood and St Irvyne would have aroused memories of that earlier time, commemorated in the poem, when she and Bysshe had first walked together in the romantic surroundings of Field Place. Her strong desire to return had been fulfilled, if only briefly and after much frustration. Now there was the further bright prospect that Bysshe would be able to follow her to London, where they might spend more days in each other's company at brother John's. In the meantime Harriet had to surrender the delights of Field Place for a brief visit to her mother's brother, Captain John Pilfold, whose wife Harriet found 'tiresome'.

During her two days at Cuckfield Harriet walked in Colonel Sergison's park and went to church, where she heard an excellent sermon. Sergison, whom they had met in London the previous year, was invited to dinner and proved to be very entertaining. Harriet observed that Charlotte 'was half in love with him'. She also noticed that he was a heavy drinker. In the belief, or hope, that he might make a suitable husband for Charlotte, a plan was made for her to return to Cuckfield on her own for a longer stay with the Pilfolds when Harriet and the rest of the family concluded their London visit and returned to Wiltshire.

That event was still a month away, however. On 21 April Mr and Mrs Grove, Charlotte, Harriet and Charles drove away from Cuckfield and arrived at Lincoln's Inn Fields to find John 'and his cat' in good health and ready to welcome them. Their first days here were spent in making social calls, doing some shopping and walking in various parts of London, including High Holborn which they soon found 'was not a fit place for us'.

Back at Field Place Shelley was preparing for the journey with his mother and Elizabeth which was to pause, on the way to Lincoln's Inn Fields, at Clapham in order to make a call at Mrs Fenning's school. This would provide an opportunity to meet his friend Edward Fergus Graham, the music teacher, who taught Shelley's younger sisters at the school and also gave Harriet music lessons while she was in London. Graham, who lived in Vine Street, Piccadilly, was a son of an old family retainer at Field Place. Shelley used him to execute various commissions in London. At the beginning of his 1810 diary Shelley recorded 'Graham for Pliny £2/15/0'. Presumably Graham had bought a copy of Pliny's *Historia*

Naturalis for Shelley who wished to make a translation of it. As soon as *Zastrozzi* was published Shelley wrote from Eton on 1 April,[2] urging Graham to bribe one or two likely reviewers. He was afraid that the publishers would take no trouble about reviews of the book, so, he wrote, 'let everything proper be done about the venal villains and I will settle with you when we meet at Easter. We will all go in a posse to the booksellers in Mr Grove's barouche and four – show them that we are no Grub Street garretters'. Continuing in this lofty vein of cynical sophistication, Shelley added,

> Pouch the reviewers – £10 will be sufficient, I should suppose, and that I can with greatest ease repay when we meet in Passion Week. Send the reviews in which *Zastrozzi* is mentioned to Field Place, the *British Review* is the hardest, let that be pouched well. My note of hand if for any larger sum is quite at your service, as it is of consequence in fiction to establish your name as high as you can in the literary lists.[3]

With his first book published while he was still at Eton, and with the alluring prospects of a few days in London and in Harriet's company, Shelley was in a buoyant mood. To arrange the meeting at Clapham he composed a joyously absurd letter to Graham, with Elizabeth as his collaborator, in a Gothic fantasia:

> My Dear Graham, – At half after twelve do you be walking up and down the avenue of trees near Clapham Church, and when you see a Post Chaise stop at Mrs Fenning's door, do you advance towards it, and without observing who are inside of it speak to them – An eventful and terrific mystery hangs over it – you are to change your name from Edward Fergus Graham to William Grove – prepare therefore for something extraordinary. There is more in a cucumber than you are aware of – in two cucumbers indeed; they are now almost 2s 6d apiece – reflect well upon that!!![4]

In a postscript Graham was given some further startling instructions:

> The Avenue is composed of vegetable substances moulded in the form of trees called by the multitude Elm trees. Elizabeth

calls them so, but they all lean as if the wind had given them a box on the ear, you therefore will know them – stalk along the road towards them – and mind and keep yourself concealed as my Mother brings a blood-stained stiletto which she purposes to make you bathe in the life-blood of her enemy.

Never mind the Death-demons, and skeletons dripping with the putrefaction of the grave, that occasionally may blast your straining eye-ball. – Persevere even though Hell and destruction should yawn beneath your feet.

For good measure Elizabeth contributed the further information that 'The fiend of the Sussex solitudes shrieked in the wilderness at midnight – he thirsts for thy detestable gore, impious Fergus'. She also explained why the letter was addressed to 'Edward Fergus H + D + Graham, Esq.': 'H + D + means Hell Devil'.

Fearing that Graham might regard the letter as wholly a spoof, with no rational content, Elizabeth switched finally to a plain, everyday style of writing:

We really expect you to meet us at Clapham in the way described by the <u>Fiendmonger</u>: should you not be able to be there in time we will call at Miller's Hotel in hopes you will be able to meet us there, but we hope to meet you at Clapham, as Vine Street is so far out of our way to L[incoln's Inn] Fields, and we wish to see you. – Your sincere Friend,

E. Shelley

More immediately, Graham was instructed to send copies of *Zastrozzi* to two of Shelley's friends, one of them being F. Dashwood at the Harley Street address of Sir J. Dashwood. It is probable that Dashwood was a fellow Etonian. Shelley's diary for 4 June contains the entry 'to go to W. Wickham with Dashwood & Leslie. Resolution made'. The Dashwoods were big landowners in Buckinghamshire, at West Wycombe.

The appointment at Clapham was arranged for Tuesday, 24 April. The next day Shelley, with his mother and his sister Elizabeth, arrived at Lincoln's Inn Fields and until their departure on 5 May Harriet enjoyed what must have been the fullest and happiest period of companionship with her acknowledged lover. In his recollection of this London visit Charles Grove commented, 'Bysshe full of life and spirits, and very well pleased with his successful devotion to my sister'.[5]

The account in Harriet's diary of their days together suffers from deletions but enough survives to give a sufficiently clear picture of how their time was spent. Much of the daytime passed in shopping expeditions. In the evenings there were dinner parties or visits to theatres. The general mood of gaiety and elation is reflected in this entry for their first day together:

> Walked in the Fields [Lincoln's Inn] with dear Bysshe then went shopping & had great fun. Left aunt & mama at Mrs Bartons & they came home in a hackney coach a shocking dirty one. Aunt S[helley] says she shall send for a chain & chain us to her. Went to the play

The desire to be *tête-à-tête*, even with the chaperoning parent, becomes transparently clear. Returning home directly the play was over ensured that 'P[ercy], Mama & myself sat up till the rest of the party came home & had a most delightful conversation'. The exchange of 'Bysshe' for 'Percy' is particularly significant. Among lovers there is a special attraction in switching from the name used in the family circle to a second neglected name which can be specially reserved for the lovers' exclusive use. After the first day of their reunion at Lincoln's Inn Fields Harriet stopped writing 'Bysshe' and referred always to 'Percy' or 'P'.

An injury to her foot made it easier for her to withdraw with Percy from the rest of the company. On 30 April she wrote, 'Staid at home all day on account of my foot the rest of the party went to the play all but Mama & Percy'; and on the following day 'Percy & I staid in doors the rest went out.'

Whatever might cloud their relationship later, there can be no doubt that at this time they delighted in each other's company as avowed lovers and were recognised as such by their parents. Aunt Shelley's joke about chaining them to her is an indication of a tolerant approval.

The glimpses of Elizabeth Shelley are interesting in view of the friendship that had developed between the two girls in their correspondence with each other. Elizabeth is seen to be highly

animated, voluble and assertive, an impression confirmed later in
the diaries of Harriet's sister, Charlotte. 'Elizabeth as noisy as ever',
is Harriet's comment now, adding later, 'Elizabeth talks and is in as
great spirits as ever'. The extent to which the two cousins were in
each other's confidence is revealed in Harriet's note on their last day
together: 'A most stupid ES has told me something that kills me with
laughing but which hinders her from coming to Tollard I am sorry
to say.'

The Groves remained in London for a further fortnight after the
departure of the Shelleys. Harriet stayed indoors a good deal and
spent time in writing. She had at least one letter from Percy,
mentioned in an entry only partially deleted. She also had a letter
from Elizabeth delivered by Mr Shelley when he came to dinner.
Graham came several times to give Harriet music lessons and her
life in general took a more domestic turn with no more theatre-
going and few daytime outings. The air of anti-climax is unmistakable. On one evening she went to the nearby house of William Long
to hear some very good singing and noted without comment that
William Helyar was among the guests. She had not seen him since
he called at Tollard two months previously.

Of greater interest in her diary at this time are the references to
her uncles John and James Pilfold and Mr Shelley. On 7 May she was
'much surprised' by the arrival of the two Pilfold uncles. After
supper 'Uncle Jem sang to us'. In the following days the uncles had
business to attend to in the city; and Uncle John went for a walk with
Charlotte, presumably to discuss the plan that she should return to
Cuckfield with him for a protracted visit and the opportunity to
become better acquainted with Colonel Sergison.

On 13 May Mr Shelley appeared and probably spent the week in
London as he twice more dined with the Groves before their visit
ended. Harriet's references to him call for a careful examination.
This is her first, on Sunday, 13 May: 'Staid in all the morning
[deletion] in the evening Mr Shelley came here he looks very unwell
[deletion]. Uncle and him shook hands and were friends during the
time he staid.' At dinner the next night Mr Shelley was, according to
Harriet, 'so pleasant, I am quite happy to see him so'; and on their
final night at Lincoln's Inn Fields she described him as 'in great
spirits'. Plainly an ominous cloud had lifted. Her implied surprise and

relief that the brothers-in-law, Timothy Shelley and John Pilfold, were reconciled after a quarrel of some sort offers a possible explanation of the mystery that surrounded the Groves' visit to Field Place. If we may assume that the primary purpose of the expedition into Sussex was to visit Mrs Grove's brother John at Cuckfield, she may have understood that an estrangement between the two men made it inadvisable to think of visiting Field Place at the same time while tempers were running high. In default of any better explanation, this would account for Mrs Grove's conviction that, at such a moment, no welcome could be expected at Field Place; in which case an invitation to Mrs Shelley to bring her two eldest children to London for a few days would be a practical alternative.

On 19 May 1810 the Groves left London. Charlotte accompanied her uncle John Pilfold to Cuckfield for a lengthy stay there. Harriet, with her parents, arrived at Tollard Royal two days later, having slept at Overton and dined in Salisbury with her brother Tom and his wife. Tom's duties with the militia made it necessary for him and Henrietta to lodge temporarily in Salisbury.

The news at Tollard was that the rector, John Helyar, was intending to move to Bath despite earlier denials. He and his wife were important and agreeable elements in the social life of the village and the thought of their departure perhaps added to Harriet's general feeling of loneliness. With Louisa away at school and Charlotte at Cuckfield, Harriet had to depend solely on Charles for companionship. In the first week after the excitements of London she was clearly dispirited. She was not a girl who indulged in self-pity, but there is no mistaking the gloom that fostered such an entry as 'Charles & I walked out for a little while, the only happiness I have here'. Charles also read to her, choosing Milton and Shakespeare's *Romeo and Juliet*. By herself she read Sterne's sermons and his *Sentimental Journey.*

Shelley meanwhile had returned to Eton for his final term, to be followed by the long summer vacation. Little is known of the detail of his life at this time except that he was strenuously pursuing a literary career in various modes, as a writer of Gothic horror novels, a thinker of radical philosophical thoughts, and a romantically languishing lover writing melancholy poems to Harriet. In her diary for the months of June, July and August Harriet gives few indications of the nature of their continuing correspondence.

Within days of her return from London she received a gift of some crayons that Shelley had commissioned Graham to despatch to her. They are not mentioned in her diary, nor is her letter of thanks, but there are deletions on 26 May and 27 May which can be correlated with Shelley's letter of the 29th sent from Eton to Graham, reporting that he had had 'a letter from Harriet this morning in which she tells me the crayons do very well'.[6] In the following week Harriet records that she made Charles 'write to Percy'. It was of course Charles who, long afterwards, affirmed that 'in the course of that summer, to the best of my recollection, after we had retired into Wiltshire, a continual correspondence was going on, as I believe there had been before, between Bysshe and my sister'.[7] For the summer months of 1810 Charles was drawing on first-hand knowledge and probably had a closer intimacy with her than at other times when the family circle was enlarged.

The month of June was dominated by a single unforeseen event which drove Harriet's normal preoccupations out of her diary. A message from Bath to say that Harriet's beloved sister Louisa, at boarding school there, was 'very unwell' with whooping cough prompted their parents to set off at once. For several days Harriet anxiously awaited their return, dining alone or with Charles. On 5 June Louisa was brought home, very weak but apparently recovering. However, the diary shows a continuing and growing alarm:

June 7. Dear Louisa & I dined together in the drawing room. Mr Wilkins has been here & rather frightened us about her. He says she must not eat meat.

June 8. Dear Louisa was kept in bed all day but is much better as her fever is gone. My father with his troop went to Devizes to quel [sic] a mutiny there amongst the local militia. We are anxious for him to return safe.

June 9. Dear Louisa told me she liked me to be with her.

June 10. Dear Louisa is still very unwell & Mr Wilkins bled her which rather frightened her. My father returned safe from Devizes.

June 11. Mr Wilkins has been here & pronounces Louisa

much better but thought it necessary to bleed her again, I am so glad to hear the dear little thing is better. I long for her to be quite well again. She is quiet.

June 12. Dear Louisa's fever as high as ever. They sent for Dr Bearwood who bled her as Mr Wilkins has three times before. I sat up with my dearest sister tonight.

The expressions of optimism and hope continue; so do the attempts to reduce the fever by bleeding. By the 17th Louisa was clearly losing ground and Harriet sat up all night with her. Next day she could write only a single sentence in her diary: 'We still have hopes of the recovery of my dear little sister'. The situation was now critical. The diary continues:

June 19. In the morning great hope but at four o'clock the dear little angel was released from her pain. What a lesson of fortitude & resignation has she left us all. I hope it may please God that I never may forget it as long as I live.

• Chapter Five •

Louisa was in her fourteenth year when she died – the same age as her sister Marianne had been when she was burnt to death four years earlier. Marianne had been the closest in age to Harriet, only a year separating them. It is quite likely that Harriet may have witnessed that tragedy when her young sister ran screaming for help, with her dress on fire. To some extent Louisa had replaced Marianne in Harriet's affections; now she too was dead. On the day she was buried Harriet ended her account of the day's events with the heartfelt cry, 'Dear Charlotte how I long to see you.' Of her four sisters Charlotte was Harriet's only remaining companion in the family house; and she was not yet due to return from Cuckfield.

It was the strong-minded authoritative presence of Aunt Grove which, in Harriet's words, 'in some degree has made us all bear our loss better'. She took them all to her home at Netherhampton for an immediate change of scene and thence to Muddiford (or Mudeford as it is now known) near Christchurch. Here they found their friends the Tregonwells, who took them to see a place Mr Tregonwell had bought as part of his plan for developing the virtually uninhabited coast of Bournemouth Bay.* 'Very barren but a pretty sea view', was Harriet's description.

For most of July the Groves remained at Muddiford for what became a family seaside holiday with the arrival of Harriet's eldest sister Emma Waddington, her husband and children; and, unexpectedly, brother William took a brief leave from his naval duties. They walked on the sands and bathed, rode in the carriage to Hordle

---

* Unlike its historical coastal neighbours – Weymouth, Poole, Christchurch and Lymington – Bournemouth is essentially a Victorian creation.

Cliffs, bought toys in Christchurch for Emma's children and collected shells with them. It was evidently a time of quiet healing, during which Harriet wrote to Aunt Shelley, to Elizabeth and to Bysshe. She does not record the receipt of any letters from them.

After the break at Muddiford the Groves delayed a return to the sad surroundings of Tollard by spending more time at Netherhampton and visiting the Waddingtons at Little Park and the Longs at Preshaw. It was the middle of August when Harriet found herself back at home and 'much rejoiced by the return of dear Charlotte and George'. Work on the new mansion at Ferne was progressing well, with the roof nearing completion, so there were frequent visits from Tollard to inspect their future home. In general her diary suggests a slackening in the correspondence with Shelley after the shared springtime days at Field Place and Lincoln's Inn Fields, though without any significant weakening in their relationship. The protracted illness of Louisa and the restless grieving movements after her funeral were hardly conducive to letter-writing. On Shelley's part it is known that during August he wrote four poems or 'Songs' which were directly addressed to Harriet or associated with her.

Two of these poems, entitled respectively 'Sorrow' and 'Hope', are conventional expressions of the unrelieved melancholy which seems genuinely to afflict adolescents for no apparent reason. 'To me this world's a dreary blank', Shelley wrote in the opening verse of 'Sorrow'; 'All hopes in life are gone and fled'.[1] In 'Hope' he found some distant consolation in an afterlife:

> Yet tho' despair my life should gloom,
> Tho' horror should around me close,
> With those I love, beyond the tomb,
> Hope shows a balm for all my woes.[2]

Set beside the actual suffering and death of Louisa the factitious gloom of these poems can hardly win much sympathy for the bright and healthy young Etonian filling in time before going up to Oxford. His voice finds a more genuine note in the 'Song' entitled simply 'To —' and starting 'Ah! sweet is the moonbeam'. The suppression of the names 'Harriet' and 'Percy' in the published version was a practice of the time that need not be preserved.

To Harriet

Ah! sweet is the moonbeam that sleeps on yon fountain,
And sweet the mild rush of the soft-sighing breeze,
And sweet is the glimpse of yon dimly-seen mountain,
'Neath the verdant arcades of yon shadowy trees.

But sweeter than all was thy tone of affection,
Which scarce seemed to break on the stillness of eve,
Though the time it is past! – yet the dear recollection,
For aye in the heart of thy Percy must live.

Yet he hears thy dear voice in the summer winds sighing,
Mild accents of happiness lisp in his ear,
When the hope-winged moments athwart him are flying,
And he thinks of the friend to his bosom so dear. –

And thou dearest friend in his bosom for ever
Must reign unalloyed by the fast rolling year,
He loves thee, and dearest one never, Oh! never
Canst thou cease to be loved by a heart so sincere.

August, 1810[3]

The other 'Song', similarly dedicated and dated, and beginning 'Stern, stern is the voice', is a variation on the same theme, with lapses into stock horror language.[4] It moves on to the same image of the 'dear voice' on the summer breeze, taking the form now of 'The last tones of thy voice on the wild breeze that swell' and it concludes with a quatrain that follows the same rhyme pattern as the other poem and has a similar final phrase:

Those tones were so soft, and so sad, that ah! never,
Can the sound cease to vibrate on Memory's ear,
In the stern wreck of Nature for ever and ever,
The remembrance must live of a friend so sincere.

Shelley probably sent some or all of these August poems to Harriet as her diary shows a deletion on 26 August, followed by an entry three days later indicating that she had written 'to Percy'. He would also have sent the poems to the printers in Worthing who were preparing a new publication entitled *Original Poetry; by Victor and*

Cazire. This was a miscellany composed by Shelley and his sister, 'Victor' being Shelley's pseudonym and 'Cazire' Elizabeth's. The bulk of the poems were Shelley's. Elizabeth's contribution included a chatty letter to Harriet in jog-trot couplets, written after their days of lively companionship in London. An odd feature of this letter is the date given at its foot – 30 April 1810. This must be wrong, as Elizabeth was in London with Harriet on that date and did not leave until 5 May. The line 'So on Friday this City's gay vortex you quit' refers to Harriet's departure from Lincoln's Inn Fields on Friday, 18 May,[5] which must put the date of Elizabeth's composition in the week commencing Sunday, 13 May. It may be significant that on 14 May Mr Shelley came to dinner at Lincoln's Inn Fields and gave Harriet a letter from Elizabeth. There is of course no knowing if this letter was in verse and in the form which was subsequently published, but it is an intriguing thought that it might have been.

The error in the date is difficult to explain except as plain carelessness. As such, it was a trivial error by comparison with the inclusion of another poem, ostensibly by Elizabeth, but already published by 'Monk' Lewis. The plagiarism was detected and Shelley blamed Elizabeth, although it is difficult to allow that he could have been deceived in a poem by a writer with whose work he was so familiar. The consequence was that *Original Poetry; by Victor and Cazire* was precipitately withdrawn, though unfortunately not before a copy had reached Tollard Royal. What was certain to give offence there was not a foolish act of plagiarism but the reference to Charlotte in Elizabeth's letter. The use of dashes to conceal names was obviously ineffective in the eyes of those who could supply them with such certainty and displeasure:

To Miss Harriet Grove
From Miss Elizabeth Shelley

For your letter, dear Harriet, accept my best thanks,
Rendered long and amusing by virtue of franks,
Tho' concise they would please, yet the longer the better,
The more news that's crammed in, more amusing the letter,
All excuses of etiquette nonsense I hate,
Which only are fit for the tardy and late,
As when converse grown flat, of the weather they talk,
How fair the sun shines – a fine day for a walk,
Then to politics turn, of Burdett's reformation,
One declares it would hurt, t'other better the nation,
Will ministers keep? sure they've acted quite wrong,
The burden this is of each morning-call song.
So Charlotte is going to Cuckfield you say,
I hope that success her great efforts will pay
That Sergison will see her, be dazzled outright,
And declare he can't bear to be out of her sight.
Write flaming epistles with love's pointed dart,
Whose sharp little arrow struck right on his heart,
Scold poor innocent Cupid for mischevious [*sic*] ways,
He knows not how much to laud forth her praise,
That he neither eats, drinks or sleeps for her sake,
And hopes her hard heart some compassion will take,
A refusal would kill him, so desperate his flame,
But he fears, for he knows she is not common game,
Then praises her sense, wit, discernment and grace,
He's not one that's caught by a sly looking face,
Yet that's *too* divine – such a black sparkling eye,
At the bare glance of which near a thousand will die;
Thus runs he on meaning but one word in ten,
More than is meant by most such kind of men,
For they're all alike, take them one with another,
Begging pardon – with the exception of my brother.
Of the drawings you mention much praise I have heard,
Most opinion's the same, with the difference of word,
Some get a good name by the voice of the crowd,

Whilst to poor humble merit small praise is allowed,
As in parliament votes, so in pictures a name,
Oft determines a fate at the altar of fame. –
So on Friday this City's gay vortex you quit,
And no longer with Doctors and Johnny cats sit –
Now your parcels arrived [?Bysshe's] letter shall go,
I hope all your joy mayn't be turned into woe,
Experience will tell you that pleasure is vain,
When it promises sun shine how often comes rain.
So when to fond hope every blessing is nigh,
How oft when we smile it is checked with a sigh,
When Hope, gay deceiver, in pleasure is drest,
How oft comes a stroke that may rob us of rest.
When we think ourselves safe, and the goal near at hand,
Like a vessel just landing, we're wrecked near the strand,
And tho' memory forever the sharp pang must feel,
'Tis our duty to bear, and our hardship to steel –
May misfortunes dear Girl, ne'er thy happiness cloy,
May thy days glide in peace, love, comfort and joy,
May thy tears with soft pity for other woes flow,
Woes, which thy tender heart never may know,
For hardships our own, God has taught us to bear,
Tho' sympathy's soul to a friend drops a tear.
Oh dear! what sentimental stuff have I written,
Only fit to tear up and play with a kitten.
What sober reflections in the midst of this letter!
Jocularity sure would have suited much better;
But there are exceptions to all common rules,
For this is a truth by all boys learnt at schools.
Now adieu my dear Harriet I'm sure I must tire,
For if I do, you may throw it into the fire,
So accept the best love of your cousin and friend,
Which brings this nonsensical rhyme to an end.

April 30, 1810[6]

Charlotte had returned to Tollard from Cuckfield in the middle of August, still a single woman and likely to remain so: Colonel

Sergison had not responded to his opportunity. In early September William embarked for the East Indies. Harriet and Charlotte, with their brothers George and Charles, paid a brief visit to Aunt Chafin Grove at Zeals before returning to Tollard where, on 16 September, Harriet's diary has a deleted passage. A reference to Shelley may be assumed, particularly in view of the following day's entry: 'Sept 17. Received the poetry of Victor & Cazire, Charlotte offended & with reason as I think they have done very wrong in publishing what they have of her.'

In the context of the generally bland tenor of Harriet's diary at this time the words 'have done very wrong' stand out with considerable force. What may have been some playful teasing privately between sisters and cousins in London before Charlotte went to Cuckfield was very different from published ridicule after the event when her disappointment still rankled. It is noticeable that Harriet refers to no other item in the book. The poems addressed to her by Shelley had presumably been seen by her already in manuscript. Now her response is solely an angry loyalty to her sister.

In the following week Harriet makes no further comment on the matter. If she wrote to Shelley or Elizabeth she did not record doing so, and no passage is deleted. She seems to be deliberately turning her attention to lighter subjects, as if to dismiss from her mind the rumblings of family indignation that must have been expressed. After a week, however, the topic comes into the open again. On 25 September Harriet wrote, 'My father had a letter from Mr S which I am sorry for, as it gives more trouble'. There can be no reasonable doubt but that 'Mr S' was Timothy Shelley.

Four days later there is a further entry in which frankness prevails, though still in a cautiously reserved way: 'In the evening my father & John entered into an argument'. To deduce the full story from such meagre details is wellnigh impossible, but it is a justifiable speculation to suggest that John Grove's affection for Elizabeth Shelley could oblige him to defend her against his father's wrath and in a more general sense to justify the ways of the Shelleys in a matter so offensive to the Groves. Time and again one comes up against the lack of any clue to the attitudes and motives of the parents, on both sides. They must always have been influential and in some respects

49

decisive, given the dependence of their children at the time, but they are too often lost to our view in a mute and shadowy obscurity. Romney has shown us what they looked like, and Timothy Shelley's growing alarm at his son's behaviour is well known, but there is nothing to amplify Charles Grove's belief that, Shelley and Grove alike, the parents at first approved the near-betrothal of Harriet and Bysshe and that the Groves later had serious misgivings. The apparent necessity for Shelley to stop addressing letters in his own person to Harriet for a period and instead to use Elizabeth as a substitute channel of communication is one mystery; another is Mrs Grove's opposition to the visit to Field Place in April and Harriet's subsequent perplexity when they arrived; a third is the parental intervention, after the publication of *Victor and Cazire*, which induced the decline and eventual extinction of the romantic engagement. In each case one sorely needs to know what agitated the collective minds of Grove and Pilfold and Shelley, for it is always worth remembering that three family loyalties and not two were involved: the Pilfold sisters, abetted by their brother John, may not always have been in accord with their husbands.

During the period of family tension caused by *Victor and Cazire* in the latter half of September and early October 1810, Harriet's brothers George, John and Charles were at home and Tom visited intermittently from Gunville; no doubt the subject was well aired. On 7 October John and Charles departed for London. There is no record of John's immediate movements, which may possibly have included a visit to Field Place to see Elizabeth and to exert whatever reconciling influence he could there.

On 21 October Harriet recorded that 'my mother heard from Aunt S'. Six days later Harriet herself heard from John and her diary entry for the following day, a Sunday, reads, 'Very wet & my father read prayers at home'. After which the rest is deleted. Shelley must have been the subject of that deleted passage, and a connection with the letter from John is a distinct possibility. Of the nature of Aunt Shelley's letter to her sister Grove one can only guess. It would not be surprising if the two wives desired to lower the temperature of their husbands' recent correspondence.

Meagre as they are, these are the last entries in Harriet's diary that refer to any of the Shelleys. During the remaining two months of 1810 nothing is deleted and there are not even any indirect signs of the stages by which the romance faltered, declined and was aborted. Harriet records an active social life in a relaxed even-tempered manner, which might lead one to suppose that November and December were two of her happiest months and that Field Place, with its personal associations, did not exist. On 28 November, for example, she wrote, 'My father's birthday. I wish he may see many happy returns of this day. George nearly killed us with laughing, he was so droll.' And when she and Charlotte went to stay for a few days with their friends the Pleydells at Whatcombe there is no doubting the hilarity and high spirits of a houseful of girls of about Harriet's age. They taught her to dance the cotillon and on 20 December she wrote, 'A very wet day & we made a great noise playing all sorts of games & danced the morning with our cotillon to a famous band. In the evening Charlotte & I acted & did all sorts of things to make them laugh.'

Evidently her diary was no longer receiving the confidences that she committed to its pages earlier in the year. In addition, she seems to have drawn back from her normally developing sexuality to the more maidenly roles of daughter and younger sister – a familiar manoeuvre in adolescence after an unpropitious encounter with reality. To discover more precisely what happened we must look elsewhere.

· *Chapter Six* ·

There are three available sources to be added to Harriet's diary in the attempt to recall and evaluate the events of the final quarter of 1810. The most circumstantial is the recollection of Harriet's brother Charles. More plainly biased is the 'official' version prepared by Shelley's daughter-in-law, Jane, Lady Shelley. These in turn are augmented by whatever is known of Shelley at the relevant time from independent biography and through his surviving letters, notably to his friend Thomas Hogg.

Charles Grove's recollection of the events of 1810, written in 1857, looked back to the family's springtime visit to Field Place and the subsequent weeks in London when Bysshe 'was full of life and spirits, and very well pleased with his successful devotion to my sister'. His account continues as follows:

> In the course of that summer, to the best of my recollection, after we had retired into Wiltshire, a continual correspondence was going on, as I believe there had been before, between Bysshe and my sister Harriet. But she became uneasy at the tone of his letters on speculative subjects, at first consulting my mother, and subsequently my father also on the subject. This led at last, though I cannot exactly tell how, to the dissolution of an engagement between Bysshe and my sister, which had previously been permitted, both by his father and mine.[1]

There is no mention of the offence given by *Victor and Cazire*, although the break is indicated as coinciding quite closely with that episode. The reference to 'speculative subjects' gains in significance from the opening sentences of Charles's next paragraph:

> In the autumn of 1810 Bysshe went to Oxford, to reside at

University College, where he became acquainted with Mr Hogg, and formed an intimate friendship with him. He found in him a kindred spirit as to his studies and speculations on various subjects, and it was not long ere Bysshe began to write on these.[2]

Lady Shelley's version, in *Shelley Memorials from authentic Sources*, is less authentic than one might expect. Bysshe and Elizabeth were dead, Harriet was not consulted or remained silent, and Lady Shelley's only source was Charles's letter, which she used rather carelessly:

> It was in the summer of this year [1809] that Bysshe fell desperately in love with his cousin, who, with her brother, was on a visit to Field Place. Elizabeth Shelley, who was then at home, always made one of their party in their moonlight strolls through the groves of Strood and the beautiful scenery of St Leonards.[3]

As we have seen, Harriet did not visit Field Place at any time in 1809. In 1810 she had one evening walk to Strood in April. If Elizabeth 'always' joined them in their moonlight strolls she must have done so in 1808 or earlier. Similarly, Bysshe's falling in love with Harriet began much earlier than the summer of 1809.

In her account of the summer of 1810 Lady Shelley relies on Charles Grove before adding some embroidery of her own:

> In the letters which passed between them after Miss Harriet Grove had returned to Wiltshire, the speculative doubts which were expressed on serious subjects alarmed the parents of the young lady for the future welfare of their daughter; and, on Shelley being expelled from Oxford, all intimacy was broken off, and Miss Grove soon made another choice. The blow fell on Bysshe with cruel force.[4]

Lady Shelley's assertions that 'all intimacy' between Bysshe and Harriet was broken off after his expulsion from Oxford – with the implied connection between the two events – and that Harriet 'soon made another choice' are untrue. He was not expelled from Oxford until 25 March 1811, when the Harriet who occupied his thoughts was not Harriet Grove but Harriet Westbrook: it was in fact Shelley who 'soon made another choice'. Later in that year, on 28 August, he married the sixteen-year-old Miss Westbrook in Edinburgh. Harriet Grove was still single and uncommitted: her betrothal to William Helyar did not take place until 3 October.[5]

Lady Shelley's reference to Shelley's 'speculative doubts' echoes Charles Grove's description of the tone of Shelley's letters 'on speculative subjects' and Tom Medwin's earlier reference to the 'sceptical' nature of the letters which aroused Felicia Hemans's complaints.* All three were using a genteel and sanitising expression as a euphemism for Shelley's very positive hostility to the Christian religion and to the institution of marriage. His radical views had been formed early, while he was still at Eton, but they were strengthened with remarkable force and rapidity on his arrival at Oxford. Here he formed a friendship of great intensity with a man who shared his basic principles, Thomas Hogg. Charles Grove, who knew them both well at this period, accurately assessed Hogg as a kindred spirit of Shelley's. The passionate alliance of the two undergraduates has an air of inevitability as it moves towards the crisis of their expulsion.

If the publication of *Victor and Cazire* had disturbed Harriet's feelings for Shelley it is certain that they would not have been calmed by the kind of letters he was likely to write to her in the autumn of 1810 when his head was full of revolutionary ideas of all sorts. None of these letters has survived, nor have any that he addressed to Mrs Hemans, but there is a further correspondence which yields a sufficiently clear impression of Shelley's letter-writing to young women 'on speculative subjects'. In the spring of 1811 he was expounding his views on religion to Harriet Westbrook, in terms that were doubtless similar to those which had distressed Harriet Grove. Of the progress and character of that correspondence a sufficiently detailed account has survived in the form of a letter written in the following year.

Writing from Dublin on 14 March 1812 to Elizabeth Hitchener, Harriet Shelley – as Miss Westbrook now was – described how she was brought up in the Christian religion, and continued:

* See p. 25.

You may conceive with what horror I first heard that Percy was an Atheist; at least so it was given out at <u>Clapham</u> [where she attended Mrs Fenning's school with Shelley's sisters]. At first I did not comprehend the meaning of the word; therefore when it was explained I was truly petrified. I wondered how he could live a moment professing such principles, and solemnly declared he should never change mine.[6]

She tried to counter Shelley's principles and for a time lived in fear of eternal punishment if she listened to his arguments. They were too strong for her, however, and her terror 'was entirely done away with'. Thanks to the force of Shelley's persuasion she could proclaim with confidence, 'My soul is no longer shackled with such idle fears'.

In this connection it is worth mentioning a recollection of Shelley at this time by one of his contemporaries, Joseph Merle, published in 1841 in *Fraser's Magazine*. Merle remarked of Shelley that 'On all other subjects he was one of the mildest and most modest youths I have ever known; but once let religion be mentioned, and he became alternately scornful and furious'.[7]

Merle also described an extraordinary plan of Shelley's to withdraw from the world with two young children, preferably female, whom he would rear in total innocence 'of religious or social government' and knowing 'nothing of men or manners' so that Shelley might eventually see 'what the impressions of the world are upon the mind when it has been veiled from human prejudice'. So original a scheme may perhaps be less original than it seems. Shelley could have adapted it from a plan conceived by Thomas Day, the author of *Sandford and Merton*. Day, an admirer of Rousseau, brought up an orphan blonde girl and a foundling brunette in absolute seclusion during the 1770s. In his case the intention was to produce in one or the other a 'child of Nature' as the perfect wife for himself, but the scheme failed to come to fruition. Shelley's later version did not get beyond the first outline.

What all this indicates is that Shelley, as yet emotionally immature but intellectually hyperactive, was choosing for himself the familiar role of the petty guru with the customary circle of docile and devout females. The two Harriets, Felicia Hemans, his sisters and later Elizabeth Hitchener were seen by him as potential initiates. In an ambiguous sentence in a letter to Hogg, interpreted variously by Shelley's biographers as referring either to Harriet Westbrook or to his sister Hellen, Shelley wrote, 'There are some hopes of this dear little girl; she would be a divine little scion of infidelity if I could get hold of her'.[8] Her identity may be uncertain* but the intention is unmistakable.

It was in this situation that Harriet Grove found herself in the late summer and early autumn of 1810. The anger aroused in September by *Victor and Cazire* would have had its effect on the general level of tolerance for Shelley's conduct of his personal correspondence with her. What an uncritical fondness might excuse would be unsettling in an atmosphere of growing alarm. The exchange of letters between the two fathers must have left an uneasiness in the Grove household about the wisdom and the extent of Harriet's intimacy with Bysshe and his sister, Elizabeth. Charles Grove suggests that Harriet took the initiative in consulting her parents, but it is at least as likely that their expressed concern and inquiries exerted a pressure which led Harriet to confide in her mother as her own misgivings mounted.

The vivacity and high spirits of the young Shelleys gave them an undeniable fascination and glamour in the eyes of their more stolid and conventional Wiltshire cousins. Charles Grove developed a close friendship with Bysshe. John Grove's frequent visits to Field Place support the view that he wanted to marry Elizabeth Shelley. Harriet must have been flattered by Shelley's verses to her and dazzled at times by his intellectual brilliance. Nevertheless, a mood of disenchantment took hold in September and October 1810, even though Harriet withheld any expression of it in her diary. The cousinly relationship had for her been richly romantic and emotionally liberating but it remained an adolescent game, a playing at love – no matter how sincere the players might be. The forward progress to marriage involved all the obstacles of prudential and practical considerations that beset any girl in Harriet's situation. Marriage, for her and her like, was virtually the only satisfactory career and way of life that was available. The choice of a spouse was therefore the one momentous decision which governed the entire future. It

---

* It is surely his sister Hellen who is intended.

was less so with men, who retained initiatives of various kinds, but for women the options were stark and plain, and normally to be resolved only after careful deliberation in which parents exerted a powerful influence. It is somewhat ironical that, at first glance, the Grove and Shelley parents would have seen an alliance between their children as conforming exactly to the accepted practice in major landowning families and would have given it their blessing accordingly. How unexpected then, and how unwelcome, was the letter-writing undergraduate of the autumn of 1810 – by turns humbly melancholic in verse and outrageously radical and almost blasphemous in prose. This was not the textbook husband of the Groves' expectations and they were denied a vision of the poet's future stature. Their counsel to Harriet to terminate or at least suspend her correspondence is easy to understand and not at all difficult to forgive, if forgiveness be required.

The precise nature of the engagement between Bysshe and Harriet that their fathers had permitted is not clear, though it may not be difficult to deduce. They were both minors, wholly dependent on their fathers, who would regard marriage as primarily an alliance of families to be made subject to the careful negotiation of a marriage settlement. Prior to that final stage, an acceptable suitor would be permitted to 'pay his addresses' to the daughter if she were willing to receive him. Within the larger family circle of cousinhood this preliminary stage would be entered with few of the obstacles that a 'stranger' might meet. In any case, the only licence given to Bysshe was to write letters to Harriet and to meet her at family gatherings supervised by the parents. There was the presumption that they might think of themselves as lovers and that a prospect of marriage at some later stage could hope for the approval of their parents.

Regency customs do not appear to offer a close analogy to the twentieth-century concept of a published act of betrothal, as a sort of declaration of intent, followed by a probationary period of engagement that might persist for many months before any formal agreement of a marriage contract. Regency fathers, having approved a proposal to which their daughter had consented, were inclined to put the negotiations between the two families in train without delay, so that the wedding followed within weeks.

The consent of the daughter would usually have been influenced by the advice, wishes and sometimes disciplinary persuasion of her father, but it was her right to give or withhold. In the extreme romantic gesture of her liberty of spirit she might vow to marry nobody but her chosen lover – as did Walter Scott's Bride of Lammermoor – and this possibility was considered by Hellen Shelley in her account of the ending of the affair:

> It was not put an end to by <u>mutual</u> consent; but both parties were very young, and her father did not think the marriage would be for his daughter's happiness. He, however, with truly honourable feeling, would not have persisted in his objection, if his daughter had considered herself bound by a promise to my brother, but this was not the case.[9]

By the end of the Michaelmas term the decision must have been made. It was in some degree foreshadowed in a poem published by Shelley during November. Entitled 'Melody to a Scene of Former Times', it is in the familiar vein of the sorrowing melancholy lover, rejected or deprived, that Shelley affected at this time in his verse-making. In its published form it appeared incongruously in *Posthumous Fragments of Margaret Nicholson*, a satirical spoof of Shelley's. Its inclusion here, rather than in the *Victor and Cazire* group where it would have been suitably placed, suggests that it was written during September or October. This in turn strengthens the likelihood that the poem may have a closer connection with reality, a more truly felt sense of rejection and accompanying grief, than the earlier ones concerning Harriet. The directness and simplicity of the opening lines seem to make a genuine response to the displeasure and censure expressed by the beloved mistress.

> Art thou indeed forever gone,
> 	Forever, ever, lost to me?
> Must this poor bosom beat alone,
> 	Or beat at all, if not for thee?
> Ah! why was love to mortals given,
> To lift them to the height of Heaven,
> Or dash them to the depths of Hell?

Yet I do not reproach thee, dear!
Ah no! the agonies that swell
   This panting breast, this frenzied brain,
Might wake my [Harriet]'s slumb'ring tear.
Oh! Heaven is witness I did love,
And Heaven does know I love thee still,
Does know the fruitless sick'ning thrill,
   When reason's judgement vainly strove
To blot thee from my memory;
But which might never, never be.
Oh! I appeal to that blest day
When passion's wildest ecstasy
Was coldness to the joys I knew
When every sorrow sunk away.
Oh! I had never lived before,
But now those blisses are no more.
   And now I cease to live again,
I do not blame thee, love; ah, no!
The breast that feels this anguished woe
Throbs for thy happiness alone.
Two years of speechless bliss are gone,
I thank thee, dearest, for the dream.
'Tis night – what faint and distant scream
Comes on the wild and fitful blast?
It moans for pleasures that are past,
It moans for days that are gone by.
Oh! lagging hours, how slow you fly!
I see a dark and lengthened vale,
The black view closes with the tomb;
But darker is the lowering gloom
That shades the intervening dale.
In visioned slumber for a while
I seem again to share thy smile,
I seem to hang upon thy tone.
   Again you say, 'Confide in me,
For I am thine, and thine alone,
   And thine must ever, ever be'.
But oh! awak'ning still anew,

Athwart my enanguished senses flew
A fiercer, deadlier agony!

Although the poem drifts into routine Gothic imagery, there is autobiographical substance in the precise reference to 'two years of speechless bliss'. The word 'speechless' has troubled some commentators, since the years 1809–10 were certainly not dumb and uncommunicative for Shelley and Harriet. I take the word, in Shelley's usage, to mean literally 'unspeakable' in the happiest sense – ineffable, indescribable. Read in that way the two years would point to the summer of 1808 as the positive start of a serious romance, a true falling in love, developing from whatever boy-and-girl encounters might have occurred since 1804.

Against the tender resignation of the poem it is instructive to set an extract from a letter written by Shelley in December 1810:

> On one subject I am cool, [religion] yet that coolness alone possesses me that I may with more certainty guide the spear to the breast of my adversary, with more certainty ensanguine it with the hearts blood of Xt's hated name.[10]

Of this letter Harriet was not the recipient, but it is a fair assumption that similar outbursts and bewildering changes of mood were to be expected of Shelley at this time and would be quite beyond her ability to contain and to accept or even tolerate. Theirs had been very much an intimacy *à deux* in a private world, almost a secret world, of love in its youthfully romantic style, compounded of long separations, brief and ecstatic moments 'of speechless bliss' in each other's company and the momentary thrills of opening a letter and composing a reply. In the small compass of such a love Harriet had certainly found happiness and might have continued to do so. For Shelley its limited scope must have become claustrophobic as his mind reached out to wider interests. To be in love might be Harriet's main preoccupation in 1810, but in Shelley's case there were competing interests. This was the year in which he launched himself with great determination as an author, the year too when his schooldays ended and at Oxford he found a new and stronger stimulation for his radical ideas. Intellectually he was outgrowing Harriet and failing to draw her into the new orbit that he was creating for himself. She had had a place in his earliest literary endeavours, but she no longer had one. Shelley's impassioned friendship with Hogg and their drafting of *The Necessity of Atheism* put an end to that.

The development of this first stage in Shelley's literary career began, according to Tom Medwin, in school vacations when they spent much time together and also corresponded.[11] In the Easter vacation of 1809, Shelley wrote to a fellow Etonian from Field Place, 'in this Solitude I have no Employment, except writing Novels & Letters'.[12] In the subsequent winter he and Medwin collaborated in writing alternate chapters of what Medwin described as 'a wild and extravagant romance, where a hideous witch played the principal part'.[13] From it they may have developed the more ambitious collaboration to write a verse-narrative, in the manner of Sir Walter Scott, on the subject of the Wandering Jew. In his 1810 diary Shelley copied passages from *Revelation*, Chapter 6, under the heading 'Wandering Jew', on the page for the week commencing 26 February.[14] He subsequently offered the poem to the publishers of Scott's poems but without success, and it did not appear in his lifetime.[15] Medwin claimed to have contributed to it.

On 11 March Shelley made an entry in his diary which signalled yet another literary endeavour. It consists of two words, somewhat carelessly written, but to be transcribed very probably as 'Began Wolfstein'. This would refer to the novel *St Irvyne or The Rosicrucian*, in which 'Wolfstein' is the name of one of the characters. The book was published before the end of the year.

In sum, therefore, 1810 was a year of strenuous effort by Shelley to win public recognition as the author of two Gothic romances (*Zastrozzi* and *St Irvyne*) and the two volumes of verse. In his first term at Oxford, in the autumn of 1810, he could expect to be regarded as a budding poet and novelist. In that role his conversations with Tom Medwin had been, in Medwin's words, 'inebriating and electric'[16] and they were certainly no less so for his new friend and collaborator at Oxford, Thomas Hogg.

The Michaelmas term, starting on 10 October, brought them together as strangers. By 17 December, when the term ended, they were the closest of friends. It would be no great exaggeration to describe their relationship as a sort of falling in love at first sight, whether or not it contained an explicitly homosexual element. On his return to Field Place for the Christmas vacation Shelley began a voluminous correspondence with Hogg. He had to wait a couple of days until Hogg gave him a temporary address in London to write to, whereupon Shelley wrote, on 20 December, 'The moment which announces your residence I write'.[17] In the course of the vacation of about a month, he wrote thirteen letters to Hogg. It has always been assumed that they contain references to Harriet, although her name is never mentioned. The presumption must therefore be made that Hogg already knew of the breakdown of Shelley's romance with his Wiltshire cousin and could therefore identify the 'she' and 'her' in Shelley's letters. It would of course have been natural for Shelley to have confided in Hogg at Oxford in the early stages of their friendship, when they opened their hearts to each other.

Nevertheless, there are some strange features in this aspect of the Christmas correspondence which merit a close examination – not least because Shelley's connection with reality at this time was at best intermittent, while Hogg did not scruple to falsify his testimony later. The passages excerpted regularly by Shelley's biographers, as evidence of Shelley's deep distress over Harriet, are as follows:

a. [20 December] Oh! I burn with impatience for the moment of Xtianity's dissolution, it has injured me; I swear on the altar of perjured love to revenge myself on the hated cause of the effect which <u>even now</u> I can scarcely help deploring. – Indeed I think it is to the benefit of society to destroy the opinions which can annihilate the dearest of its ties.

b. [1 January] I am but just returned to F[ield] P[lace] from an inefficient effort. Why do you my happy friend tell me of perfection in love, is she not gone —

c. [3 January] Oh how I wish I <u>were</u> the Antichrist, that it <u>were</u> mine to crush the Demon, to hurl him to his native Hell never to rise again – I expect to gratify some of this insatiable feeling in Poetry. You shall see, you shall hear. – but it has injured me, she is no longer mine, she abhors me as a Deist, as what <u>she</u> was before.

d. [6 January] Forsake her! forsake one whom I loved! can I? never – but she is gone, she is lost to me forever, forever.

e. [11 January] She is gone, she is lost to me forever – she is married, married to a clod of earth, she will become as insensible herself, all those fine capabilities will moulder.[18]

Taking these excerpts at face value, they imply (a) that Harriet's Christian faith compels her to perjure their vows of love and break the 'dearest of ties'; (b) that Shelley, in his desire for reconciliation, has made a somewhat mysterious journey, which achieved (c) nothing; (d) and (e) that the break is final because she has married someone else, much inferior to herself culturally. On this last point Thomas Love Peacock tried to rationalise the words 'she is married' by suggesting that Shelley had heard that Harriet had become engaged to William Helyar.[19]

There is one further letter to Hogg which greatly influenced earlier biographers in their attempts to reconstruct the manner in which the romance was terminated by Harriet. I shall give two versions of it, for a reason that will become apparent. According to Hogg, the letter written to him by Shelley on 23 December reads:

My sister [Elizabeth] attempted sometimes to plead my cause, but unsuccessfully. She [Harriet] said:

'Even supposing I take your representation of your brother's qualities and sentiments, which as you coincide in and admire, I may fairly imagine to be exaggerated, although <u>you</u> may not be aware of the exaggeration; what right have <u>I</u>, admitting that he is so superior, to enter into an intimacy which must end in delusive disappointment, when he finds how really inferior I am to the being which his heated imagination has pictured?'

This was unanswerable, particularly as the prejudiced description of a sister, who loves her brother as she does, might indeed <u>must</u>, have given to her an erroneously exalted idea of the superiority of my mental attainments.[20]

It is in that form that the letter appears in Hogg's own biography of Shelley. It is not, however, in the form that Shelley wrote; nor are the discrepancies it contains minor inaccuracies of transcription. It is, to be blunt, a forgery. What Shelley wrote had nothing to do with

Harriet's rejection of himself, but with his sister Elizabeth's rejection of Hogg.

Unwisely, as it turned out, Shelley had sought to promote a love match between Elizabeth and Hogg. No doubt in his first infatuation with Hogg, Shelley had wanted to strengthen the bonds that united them by offering Hogg this added alliance. Hogg's amused, patronising, man-of-the-world attitude to Shelley when, in middle age, he wrote *The Life of Percy Bysshe Shelley* does not represent his feelings in 1810, which seem to have fed on a mixture of hero-worship and romantic posturing. Though he never met Elizabeth Shelley, and only once, at a later date, saw her fleetingly, he embarked instantly on an impassioned courting of her by letter. In effect, he made her his equivalent of Shelley's Harriet.

Elizabeth's uncompromising refusal even to read Hogg's letters made Shelley strive to cool his friend's ardour. It was in this bizarre situation that Shelley wrote his letter of 23 December, the authentic text of which did not become potentially available until 1948 when it was sold at auction by a member of the Hogg family.[21] In 1961 it was published in *Shelley and His Circle*, where Kenneth Neill Cameron collated it with the version in Hogg's biography of Shelley and examined the significance of Hogg's alterations. These, in Cameron's judgment, 'misrepresented a series of events and relationships and misled succeeding biographers';[22] and they did so deliberately.

Elizabeth Shelley's intervention with Harriet Grove is a myth created by Hogg. Purged of his 'editing', the relevant part of the letter of 23 December reads as follows:

I have attempted again to plead your cause but unsuccessfully. She [Elizabeth] said – 'even supposing I take your representation of your friends qualities & sentiments which as you coincide in & admire I may fairly imagine to be exaggerated altho' you may not be aware of the exaggeration, what right have I admitting that he is so superior to enter into a correspondence which must end in delusive disappointment when he finds how really inferior I am to the being which his heated imagination had pictured' – This was unanswerable, particularly as the prejudiced description of a brother who loves his sister as I do, may, indeed must have given to you an erroneously exalted idea of the superiority of her mental attainments.[23]

So it came about that more than a hundred years after these events Shelley's biographers still believed, understandably, that Elizabeth Shelley interceded with Harriet to save her brother's romance; and that Harriet rejected him and immediately pledged herself to Helyar. That was Hogg's interpretation based on Shelley's letters written to him and 'edited' by him. It became the accepted, recognised truth.

And truth is what it certainly was not.

· *Chapter Seven* ·

On Christmas Day 1810 Harriet Grove wrote in her diary, 'Bought pocket book for next year'. In that context 'pocket book' is synonymous with 'diary'; there is no reason to doubt that she continued to record each day's events as she had done in previous years. The loss of her 1811 book is unfortunate. At some point it was separated from those for 1809 and 1810 which were sold at auction for the collectable nature of the Shelley references they contained. The disposal of her diaries is examined in Appendix One.

The disappointing silence that falls on Harriet's testimony on 31 December 1810 is in some measure compensated by my discovery of a companion volume – I might say a sister volume – which picks up on the following day, 1 January 1811. This is the earliest survivor of a long run of diaries written by Harriet's elder sister, Charlotte. It styles itself 'The complete Pocketbook or Gentleman's and Trades-man's Journal', and on its fly-leaf Charlotte has written, 'I bought this at Salisbury'. With this and her subsequent pocket books, she becomes the chronicler of Grove family life in Wiltshire after 1810 and of the continuing association with the Shelleys at Field Place, particularly with Elizabeth. More immediately, she helps to clarify and supplement the version of the Christmas vacation provided by Shelley's letters and Hogg's biography. With the addition of Charles Grove's recollections, the following reconstruction emerges.

On 18 December 1810, Shelley returned to Field Place from Oxford.[1] A letter of his, dated 2 December, to Stockdale, the publisher of *St Irvyne*, suggests that Shelley intended to break his journey homeward in London and call on Stockdale.[2] If to do so necessitated an overnight stay in London he could have joined his cousins, John and Charles, at Lincoln's Inn Fields, having Charles as his companion next day on the coach to Horsham. Charles in his own account says, 'During the Christmas vacation of that year [1810], and in January 1811, I spent part of it with Bysshe at Field Place'.[3] As he returned to Wiltshire for the family's New Year celebrations, probably arriving on 28 December,[4] it is at least a reasonable assumption that he accompanied Bysshe to Field Place at the start of the vacation.

What adds colour to this is an action of Shelley's. On 18 December, the day of his return, Shelley wrote to Stockdale giving him instructions to despatch advance copies of *St Irvyne* to a Miss Marshall in Horsham, to Hogg at a visiting address and to Tom Medwin.[5] There was no mention of Harriet or any other Grove. However, Charlotte's diary includes an entry for 5 January: 'Read Bysshe's new novel', which must suggest that Charles had been given a copy or entrusted with one to deliver to Harriet, and for that reason Shelley had not instructed Stockdale to send one to Tollard Royal.

The entry for 28 December in Harriet's diary begins, 'My brothers came joyful event, George more noisy than ever'. She did not name the other brothers individually. Two can be ruled out: William was on naval duty in the East Indies, and Tom was permanently resident in the vicinity, at Littleton near Blandford. His wife, Henrietta, had invited all the available brother and sister Groves to a dance on New Year's Day.[6] John Grove is mentioned incidentally by Harriet on the 29th and must have been one of the brothers who arrived on the 28th, and I have no doubt that Charles accompanied him. By his own account, his visit to Field Place was in two parts – 'during the Christmas vacation of that year, and in January 1811' – and he was certainly at Tollard Royal over the New Year period. The entry in Charlotte's diary for 5 January reads, 'My brothers John, George & Charles walked to aunt Jackson's and slept there'. They returned next day in time for dinner and possibly heard Charlotte's opinion of Bysshe's *St Irvyne or The Rosicrucian*, which she had read while they were visiting the Jacksons at Donhead St Mary. The comment she wrote in her diary was 'Great stuff'. Some caution is required in deciding what precisely the word *stuff* meant in the vocabulary of a well-bred young Regency woman – not, I think, as flattering as a first impression might suggest.

On 7 January Charlotte and Harriet walked with their father to

Ferne to see how work on the new mansion was progressing. Later that day John, Charles and Mr Grove 'set out for London'. With a further eight hours in the coach from London to Horsham, Charles would have arrived at Field Place on the 9th at best, though equally he might have stayed in London temporarily. That he did return to Field Place is not in doubt. When the time came for Shelley to start the new term at Oxford he was accompanied by Charles from Field Place to London where they went together to visit a schoolfriend of Shelley's sister Mary, to deliver a gift from Mary.[7] The general picture of Charles's movements in this period is that he was invited to Field Place to provide congenial companionship for Bysshe during the Oxford vacation, but did not wish to miss the usual Grove family reunion at New Year which, rather than Christmas, was the occasion for exchanging gifts and mustering at full strength. As he was very much in the care of his brother John, and was residing with John at Lincoln's Inn Fields, he accompanied his brother to Tollard Royal and back to London.

This assembly of Grove evidence – the diaries of the two sisters and Charles's recollections – should finally lay to rest the notion that, around New Year's Eve, Shelley made a desperate, direct bid for a reconciliation with Harriet. Its source is in the letters written to Hogg in the first days of 1811, where the following passages occur:

[1 January] I am but just returned to FP from an inefficient effort. Why do you my happy friend tell me of perfection in love, is she not gone —[8]

[6 January] I have tried the methods you recommend. I followed her, I would have followed her to the end of the earth but —.[9]

In 1811, 1 January was a Tuesday. In the course of his letter to Hogg on that day, Shelley says he departed from Field Place on Sunday morning. This suggested to earlier biographers that he might have travelled to Tollard Royal to plead with Harriet, and have been rebuffed. I doubt if it would even have been possible to make the return journey by stagecoach in forty-eight hours, but it is inconceivable that both Harriet and Charlotte would have omitted to mention such a remarkable intrusion on 31 December if it had happened.

This is Harriet's record of that day:

> I wish my father would give us our allowance. John Gordon left us this morning. I gave him some country dances for the band at Shaftesbury. We danced in the evening. Daniel played the violin & Wm the tamborine to us. We are very much afraid the snow will prevent us from going to Littleton tomorrow.[10]

Daniel, who played the violin for dancing, was a senior member of the house staff, Daniel Lampard. 'Wm' was a servant, deputising for Mrs Grove, who sometimes liked to take the tambourine herself and accompany Daniel's violin.

Charlotte's entry for 1 January reads: 'We went to Lyttleton & left my Father & Mother at home. A Dutch concert the whole way.* Henrietta greeted us most cordially.' An additional note written by Charlotte on a fly-leaf supplements this spare account with some more vivid detail:

> 1st   We had a very pleasant dance at my brother's house: <u>5</u> Miss Pleydells, 2 Miss Williams's, Miss Tregonwell & Miss Bastard. Mr Gibbs, Bryne, Dansey & Stewarts were the dancers. Miss T was <u>dressed</u> like a <u>bride</u>. Harriet, George & myself danced a cotillon with the Miss Pleydells, dear charming friends of ours. Henrietta called a cousin of hers a goose.[11]

The relaxed holiday mood of the two sisters could not have been so patently unruffled if Shelley had indeed 'followed' Harriet. An ingenious alternative for his 'inefficient effort' has been suggested by Kenneth Neill Cameron who considered that Shelley might have gone, not to Tollard Royal, but to London to ask Charles Grove to plead for him.[12] All that is known of Charles's movements contradicts this; and in any case Shelley could have enlisted Charles's sympathy and help while they were together at Field Place a few days earlier. A visit to the house in Lincoln's Inn Fields on 30 or 31

---

* A Dutch concert is one in which each performer plays a different tune (OED).

December would, I am convinced, have found nobody at home except John's housekeeper and his cat.

Is there any other possibility? One cannot rule out an appeal to Uncle John Pilfold at Cuckfield. He filled the role of a father to Bysshe, according to Tom Medwin, and Harriet Grove was his sister's child. The possibility remains. In default, Shelley's words add to the bewilderment generated by his letters to Hogg during the Christmas vacation.

There are two features of these letters that must strike a reader today as strange. One is the atmosphere of solitary confinement, self-imposed, which almost eliminates the living context of Field Place. The other is the astonishingly abrupt changes of topic, mood and emotional intensity. Despite the quantity and length of Shelley's letters to him, Hogg would have gained almost no idea of how his friend passed his time, and in what company, when he was not writing letters. There is a passing reference to 'all the uncongenial jollities of Xmass [sic]'; a mention of Shelley's going for a walk to overcome sleepiness; and some family discord when Shelley becomes involved in a religious debate with his father, and his mother – in Shelley's words – 'fancies me in the High Road to Pandemonium, she fancies I want to make a deistical coterie of all my little sisters'.[13]

Those little sisters – Mary, aged thirteen, Hellen, eleven, and Margaret, ten – participated in nothing with him that he chose to communicate to Hogg. More surprisingly, there is not the merest mention of the presence of Harriet's brother Charles Grove. Had there been, Hogg must have found it difficult to comprehend how such an equable and undisturbed friendship could co-exist with the peak of distress caused by Harriet's 'perjury' of the love vows. It might have been supposed that the straining of the relationship between the two families would have made Charles a singularly inappropriate guest at Field Place; yet in truth the friendship between Charles and Bysshe was never stronger than in the winter and spring of 1811.

In his letters to Hogg Shelley was mainly preoccupied with four recurring themes: their literary endeavours; their larger religious and philosophical attitudes; Hogg's infatuation with the – to him – unknown and unknowable Elizabeth Shelley; and Shelley's disappointed love for an unnamed woman assumed to be Harriet Grove. The last-mentioned topic is given much less prominence and a more fragmentary treatment than might be imagined by anyone who has not read the letters in full. To give one example immediately, I will quote, without abridgement, an early part of Shelley's letter of 20 December in which he is advising Hogg on how to find a publisher for *Leonora*, a novel containing opinions of Hogg's which conventional publishers like Stockdale would fear to publish because of their heretical nature:

> Stockdale will no longer do for me; I am at a loss whom to recommend; S[tockdale]'s scull [*sic*] is very thick but I am afraid that he will not believe your assertion, indeed should it gain credit with him, should he accept the offer on publication there exist numbers who will find out its real tendency, & booksellers possess more power than we are aware of, in impeding the sale of any book whose opinions are displeasing to them – I would recommend offering it to Wilkie & Robinsons/ Paternoster Row, & to take it there yourself, he publishes Godwin's works, it is scarcely possible to suppose than [that] anyone but a Clergyman would assert that it supported the doctrines of the Gospel – if that will not do, I would recommend you to print it yourself; Oxford of course would be more convenient for the correction of the press – Mr Munday's principles are not <u>very</u> severe, – he is more a votary to Mammon than God. – Oh! I burn with impatience for the moment of Xtianity's dissolution, it has injured me; I swear on the altar of perjured love to revenge myself on the hated cause of the effect which <u>even now</u> I can scarcely help deploring. – Indeed I think it is to the benefit of society to destroy the opinions which <u>can</u> annihilate the dearest of its ties. – Inconv[en]iences would now result from my <u>owning</u> the novel which I have in preparation for the press. I give out therefore that I will publish no more; every one here, but the select few who enter into its schemes believe my assertion – I will stab the wretch in secret. —[14]

The step from Mr Munday's lax principles to Christianity's annihilation of the romantic tie with Harriet is so precipitate and inconsequential as to seem almost an irrelevant aside: he returns immediately to the problem of finding a way to publish his subversive writings. Subsequently the letter runs on at considerable length with no further sign of interest in Harriet. She – or some other unnamed person – had aroused just that one momentary digression.

Even more remarkable in its unheralded interruption of a wholly unrelated topic is the letter of 6 January, which begins with Shelley's appeal to Hogg to refrain from writing love letters to Elizabeth, who cannot respond since she has no acquaintance of him:

My dear Friend,

Dare I request <u>one</u> favour – for <u>myself</u> for my own interest not the keenest anguish which the most unrelenting Tyrant could invent should force me to request from you so great a sacrifise [*sic*]. – It is a beloved sister's happiness which forces me to this. I saw her when she received your letter of yesterday. I saw the conflict of her soul, she said nothing but re-directed it, & sent it instantly to the Post. Believe me I feel for you more than I will <u>allow</u> myself to perceive for any disap[p]ointments which I have undergone. Write to me – whatever you wish to say to Eliza you may say in that, and she might by a brother's wish what in the other case I dared not even to recommend. What would I not give up to see you, to see my sister happy. I know the means by which it can be effected, but consider what a female sacrifises [*sic*] when she returns the attachment of one whose faith she supposes inviolable even. To add to the agony which is indescribable, which is only to be felt will she not encounter the opprobrium of the world, and what is more severe (generally speaking) the dereliction & contempt of those who before had avowed themselves most attached to her. – <u>I</u> do not encourage the remotest suspicion, I am convinced of your truth as I am of my own existence, still is [it] not <u>Natural</u> in Eliza even altho she may return the most enthusiastic prepossessions [?arising] from the consciousness of your intellectual superiority, ignorant as she is of your <u>every</u> opinion, <u>every</u> sensation (for <u>unlimited</u> confidence is requisite for the existence of mutual love) to have some doubts, some fears. Besides when in her natural character, her spirits are good her conversation animated, & almost in consequence ignorant of the refinements in Love, wch. can only be attained by solitary reflexion. – Forsake her! forsake one whom I loved! can I? never – but she is gone, she is lost to me forever, forever. There is a mystery which I dare not to clear up, it is the only point on which I will be reserved to you. – I have tried the methods you recommend. I followed her, I would have followed her to the end of the earth but –. If you value the little happiness which yet remains, do not mention again to me sorrows which if you could share in, would wound an heart which it now shall be my endeavour to heal from those which it has already received.[15]

The words 'Forsake her!' must in all reason be read at first as applying to Elizabeth. It is only gradually that what follows makes it clear that Shelley's thoughts have switched abruptly to someone else, since he can hardly be talking about following his sister to the end of the earth when she is sitting beside him at Field Place.

The other key outburst, which is always interpreted as a reference to Harriet, occurs in an even more chaotic fashion. This is in a letter to Hogg dated 11 January which again is primarily concerned with Elizabeth's immediate return, unread, of Hogg's latest letter to her. Increasingly desperate in his attempts to stifle Hogg's courtship, Shelley produces a high-flown version of Elizabeth's own words. With the omission of the opening sentences, which are merely tedious, the letter reads:

How can I find words to express my thanks for yr. mild, yr. generous conduct with regard to my Sister; with susceptibilities such as your own, yet to promise what I ought not to have required, what nothing but a dear Sisters peace could have induced me to demand. – Pardon me; believe that the first wish of my heart is that against wch. I seem to be acting in opposition – when yr. letter came and my sister <u>instantly</u> returned it, what arguments did I leave unused to induce her to recall the Servant who took it. She was deaf to every solicitation. 'Reason, Virtue, Justice forbade it, as <u>yet</u> she was

uninfluenced by passion, as yet she wd. follow the dictates of
that Reason which was unimpaired by awakened susceptibilities, he wd. be disappointed in me, most <u>bitterly</u> so. I will not
read it.' I, even I̲ a brother did not see the force of her
Reasoning, I submitted, submitted to what I knew must inflict
a most cruel pang. Religion! this is thy remote influence. –
What can I say on the subject of yr. letter to Eliza, is it not
dictated by the most generous of human motives, & yet I have
not shewn it to her. Need I explain the reason? – It is the only
thing on which I will make the least cloud of mystery, it is the
only point on which I will be a solitary being – to be solitary, to
be reserved in communicating pain surely cannot be criminal,
it cannot be contrary to the most strict duties of friendship.
She is gone, she is lost to me forever – she is married, married
to a clod of earth, she will become as insensible herself, all those
fine capabilities will moulder. Let us speak no more on the
subject. Do not deprive me of the little remains of peace which
yet linger, that which arises from endeavours to make others
happy —[16]

There is once more the ambiguity of 'she' in a sudden change of
identity. Elizabeth is not married, to a clod of earth or anything else:
yet the letter, up to this point, has been exclusively about her. If
not Elizabeth, then, who was the bride? In default of any other
candidate, commentators have assumed that Shelley was referring
to Harriet and have tried to explain away the word 'married'. What
Shelley *meant*, so the argument goes, is that Harriet had now agreed
to marry William Helyar, had become formally engaged to him.[17]
Peacock ingeniously suppressed the word 'is' and explained that 'she,
married!' was an exclamation of outrage at such a wretched prospect
but need not imply that it had already happened. What no one knew
was when in fact Harriet did become engaged to Helyar; and what
no one seems to have suspected is that it was not until after Shelley's
own marriage.[18]

To do justice to Shelley, though, in the immediate context of his
letter of 11 January it is proper to recall that Charles Grove would
just have returned to Field Place, bringing with him the latest gossip
from his family at Tollard Royal. At the time of his departure

Charles would have heard Charlotte and Harriet discussing the annual ball at Shaftesbury, which was to be held on 8 January – the day after he set off to London with his brother John and their father. It had been at the Shaftesbury ball a year ago* that Harriet had enjoyed partnering William Helyar and she may have been looking forward to a renewal of that pleasure. It was certainly hoped for by Charlotte, who was an inveterate matchmaker where her brothers and remaining sister were concerned. She had seen Harriet and William together in the last months of 1809 and must have decided that he was locally the most eligible husband for her sister.

The year 1810 had not developed in the way Charlotte would have liked. William Helyar is mentioned only twice in Harriet's diary during the whole of the year. In March he called unexpectedly at Tollard just before Harriet and Charlotte set off on a walk they had planned. In May there was a meeting by chance as fellow guests at a dinner party in London. After May 1810 Harriet made no reference to William in her diary. It may be worth mentioning that, in accordance with social etiquette, she distinguishes him from his father, his uncle and his brothers by the use of his initial or Christian name. An entry using the form 'Mr Helyar', simply, would indicate the head of the family, William's father.

From what may be learned of Charlotte's character from her diary, it is easy to imagine that there was some teasing of Harriet about the likelihood that 'Billy' might be at the Shaftesbury ball, as he had been at the previous one. Something of the kind had happened then, when Mary Shelley wrote to Louisa Grove about a rumour of Harriet's impending marriage at that time (see Chapter Three). The invention of romances, love affairs, betrothals and accompanying gossip is part of the fun of maidenhood.

It may be that something of the sort, reported by Charles on his return to Field Place, sparked off Shelley's astonishing outburst. Considering his correspondence with Hogg in general, it is difficult not to conclude that, in the main, he was striving to impress his friend by striking audacious and noble attitudes and revelling in emotional crises, which were confined to the closet where he wrote the letters and which evaporated when he left his writing bureau.

* 22 December 1809 (see p. 24)

Both of them seem to have put a great deal of effort into self-dramatisations, without permitting reality to impede them.

To return prosaically to the Shaftesbury ball, one's sense of the ironies of life is enriched by Charlotte's account of how it all turned out. 'Not many people', she wrote, 'and very freezing cold'.[19] It was a time of hard frosts, bitterly cold winds and falls of snow.

Two days later she could write in a happier vein. After staying with their friends the Gordons, who had escorted them to Shaftesbury, they moved on to join a house party as the guests of John Benett at Pythouse, between Tisbury and East Knoyle. Benett became a member of Parliament in 1819 and represented Wiltshire for twenty-five years, earning a disagreeable fame as 'Gallon Loaf' Benett in William Cobbett's savage attacks on him. Now, in 1811, he had been married for ten years, had a son aged one and a half, and was entertaining friends and neighbours. Among the guests were the Helyars from nearby Sedgehill, prompting Charlotte to comment in her diary, 'I am in hopes from circumstances of what I have long wished taking place'.[20] This implies that one of 'the Helyars' present was William. His brother Harry called at Pythouse the following day.

For the rest of January Charlotte and Harriet remained at home, playing battledore and chess, and having as their principal companion Helen Tregonwell, on a visit to them from Cranborne. Their youngest brother George had remained behind when John and Charles returned to London, but he too went away a fortnight later to join his ship. It was an uneventful period. Even so, Charlotte's observant style and outgoing nature give a sprightliness to her account, and her matchmaking propensity runs on:

January 24. The King is better. I hope he will be well before the Regency takes place.

January 26. Harriet & I sent up the box of books to London. I stumbled in pattens, thought I had broke my leg, stuck in the mud. Helen hung in a hedge like a petticoat hung out to dry.

January 27. Went to morning church & staid an hour & half before Mr Ridout [the curate] came in. Walked afterwards with Miss Tregonwell & Harriet.

January 28. Miss T [Helen Tregonwell] Harriet & I walked to Ferne. Met Henrietta [Tom's wife] in the Cottage Lane. Saw 6 foxhunters at Fern. Mr Farquharson took us for witches. On our return found Mr H. Helyar at Tollard. A disappointment – H[arriet] thought it was <u>Billy</u>. He dined & slept here. We acted, sang etc. to him. He brought us a song of Handell's.

January 29. Mr Henry Helyar left us. We are invited to Sedgehill as soon as the Waddingtons have left us. May our visit be productive of everything I wish & much pleasure.

January 30. I gave Helen a pocket book for the year. Helen, Harriet & I took a walk and built castles in the air. May they have a strong foundation before the summer. Tried Handell's songs – too fine for us.

January 31. Harriet & I acted Mrs Prim & Mrs Lovely & made Daddy & Mummy laugh a lot.

February 1. Charles Jackson & Hugh Helyar called. The former [their cousin] has charming manners. The latter [William's youngest brother] is very shy indeed.

February 2. Our dear friend Helen went home. She ran away with my young Roscius. We saw Mr J. Helyar's servant at the cottage. Harriet knew the livery directly.

February 3. Susan* related something of Ld & Lady Arundell. I hope it is not true.

February 4. My mother rode to Rushmore. Mr William Helyar called on us. Joked me about my acting. We could not prevail on him to stay. The books came from Town.

February 6. Miss F. Benett came. We acted to her in the evening.

February 7. We shewed Miss Benett King John's Palace. She admired it & wished to live there.

---

* A maidservant at Ferne.

February 8. [Friday] The fair Catholick fasted. H[arriet] & I took her blowing her nose for some of her devotions. H[arriet] thought she was whipping herself.

February 9. Miss F. Benett went home. My father hunted so late that we did not dine till 7 o'clock & it made us very sleepy.

February 10. My birthday – 28.[21]

· *Chapter Eight* ·

At Field Place the Christmas and New Year holiday came to an end, so far as Shelley and Charles Grove were concerned, on or about 21 January 1811 when they travelled to London together. Shelley's further destination was Oxford, where he expected to arrive on the 24th or 25th. Charles remained in London, at his brother's residence in Lincoln's Inn Fields, where he continued to prepare himself for a medical career. A few weeks later, at the beginning of March, he paid 6 guineas to attend St Bartholomew's Hospital, where he was to walk the wards for six months under the instruction of Ludford Harvey.

Before they left Field Place, Mary Shelley asked Bysshe to do something on her behalf in London: to deliver a gift to one of the friends she had made at the Clapham school. As Charles Grove recalled, '... his sister Mary sent a letter of introduction with a present to her school fellow, Miss Westbrook, which Bysshe and I were to take to her. I recollect we did so, calling at Mr Westbrook's house'.[1]

On the face of it, there is nothing remarkable about such a commission; nevertheless a couple of questions arise. The new term at Mrs Fenning's school must have been on the point of starting, with Harriet Westbrook and Hellen Shelley among the pupils reassembling at Clapham. Mary Shelley's presence is not attested but she would not have left the school because of her age. In January 1811 she was thirteen and a half, two years younger than her friend, Miss Westbrook. The obvious course would have been to take the gift herself, or – if she were not able to do so – to entrust it to Hellen. I have no doubt this would have been made plain to her by her brother if he had considered it an irksome obligation to undertake himself. What becomes more plausible is that he welcomed, or even

contrived, this opportunity to call on the schoolgirl whose acknowledged beauty could have been an added incentive. To prepare her for
his arrival, and to give her a preliminary sense of his accomplish-
ments, on 11 January he instructed the publisher of *St Irvyne* to send
her a copy of the book.[2] There was nothing casual about the visit, as
he revealed months later in a letter written to Elizabeth Hitchener
on 28 October 1811:

> Some time ago when my Sister [Mary] was at Mrs Fenning's
> school, she contracted an intimacy with Harriet [Westbrook] –
> at that period I attentively watched over my sister, designing if
> possible to add her to the list of the good, the disinterested, the
> free. – I desired therefore to investigate Harriets character, for
> which purpose, I called on her, requested to correspond with
> her designing that her advancement should keep pace with,
> and possibly accelerate that of my sister.[3]

His mother's suspicion at the time that Shelley was aiming to make
a 'deistical coterie' of his sisters was evidently well founded.

Before he left home Shelley had given instructions to the printers
at Worthing, who had produced the ill-fated *Victor and Cazire* volume,
to undertake a new job for him – a little pamphlet of about half a
dozen pages of text entitled *The Necessity of Atheism*. Written in
collaboration with Hogg, this was to be delivered to Oxford for
distribution to clerics whom Shelley wished to engage in contro-
versy. He also decided to put it on sale to the public, with
consequences which led to his and Hogg's expulsion from the
university.

While at Oxford he was also starting a correspondence with
Harriet Westbrook, who was now to replace Harriet Grove as the
object of his solicitude. Meanwhile, at Tollard Royal cousin Harriet's
life was taking an unexpected turn. It had been suggested that the
invitation to Charlotte and herself to make their first visit to the
Helyars at Sedgehill should be taken up when their sister Emma
Waddington and her family concluded their stay at Tollard. However, the departure of the Waddingtons cleared the way for a visit of
a very different sort. Aunt Chafyn Grove had made arrangements
for an extended stay at Bath and requested that Charlotte and
Harriet should join her there.[4]

Aunt Chafyn, as she was known within the family, was a Grove both by birth and by marriage. Thomas Grove senior was her brother. Her husband, William, was the head of the junior branch of the family, the Chafyn Groves of Zeals. As a Member of Parliament, William Chafyn Grove represented Shaftesbury and Weymouth before his death in 1793 left Aunt Chafyn a wealthy childless widow.[5] Her invitation to her two nieces, with or without the prompting of their parents, may have been occasioned by the thought that their abortive romances in the previous year made a complete change of scene desirable. At Bath, under the patronage of their aunt, they would meet a whole new circle of acquaintances.

Their final day at Tollard was 28 February. 'In a bustle, packing up', Charlotte wrote. 'A great event to us rusticks'. Next day they arrived at Bath 'just as it was dark'. The route from Tollard took them through Sedgehill. As they passed the Helyar residence they saw two ladies in red cloaks, walking, and some other ladies and gentlemen came out of the house when they recognised the Grove livery.[6]

Among the fashionable crowds at Bath there were a few familiar faces – some of their Long and Rudge kinsfolk, Wiltshire neighbours like the Penruddocks and the rector of Tollard Royal, the Rev. John Helyar, who had moved permanently to Bath. Making social calls, drinking tea and visiting the Pump Room occupied Charlotte and Harriet for much of the daytime. In the evening there were routs, theatre-going, concerts and dancing. Despite these activities, Charlotte found time to keep her diary up to date and preserve a record of the more memorable pleasures and disappointments during their five weeks' stay:

March 12. We went with Mrs Armswick to the play 'The Foundling of the Forest'. A gentleman impertinently wished to get acquainted with me.

March 14. Practised cotillons in the morning. A Mr Riman hid himself & we could not dance it. I danced in Miss Dalrymple's set. Harriet danced country dances. A Mr Cratton rather struck with her.

March 18. In the evening to Mrs Jekyll's rout – stupid enough. To the ball afterwards which we liked. I danced before

tea with Mr Willoughby, afterwards with a gentleman introduced by Mr King & Mrs Marsh, our chaperone.

March 19. Went to the ball at the Lower Rooms. Danced
with Mr Brock & a gentleman introduced by Mr Cratton.
Harriet danced with Mr Cratton all the evening.

March 21. Fagging about our cotillons in the morning.
Disappointed in the evening. A stupid hot ball. Danced country
dances with Mr Roos.

March 23. Walked out with Miss Marsh & Mr Cratton. Saw
Jagger's miniatures. A likeness of Mr King so striking. Met a
madman & his attendant.

March 25. Went to the Upper Rooms. Mr King introduced
me to a Mr Scott, a very gentlemanlike man with whom I
danced country dances before tea. He is engaged as my partner
for cotillons.

March 28. Practised in the morning & danced cotillons in the
evening – my partner, Mr Scott. Many young ladies wished to
be introduced to him.

March 31. Col. Peachy whom we met gave us a treble How
d'ye do.

April 1. Went to the pleasantest rout at Mrs Parker's.
Introduced to several beaux. Went to the ball, danced with a
vulgar partner. Preferred the rout.

April 2. We went to the Lower Rooms. I am nearly tired of
dancing. Mrs Merrick nearly lamed me.[7]

There were quieter evenings also when the two girls stayed at
home with Aunt Chafyn and acted to her or read to her from a copy
of Scott's *Marmion* which Charlotte had bought as a gift for her
father. The mutual liking of Harriet and Mr Cratton for each other's
company was shortlived, and Charlotte soon lost sight of the
popular Mr Scott among the bevy of young ladies surrounding him.

One of William Helyar's brothers was in Bath, visiting his uncle
and aunt, but could not be persuaded to dance cotillons. William,
who surely would have done so, remained at Sedgehill. There, out
walking with a local clergyman, he had a chance meeting with
Charlotte and Harriet as they drove home to Tollard Royal on 6
April.

On the first evening after their return Charlotte noted 'a very pleasant conversation after dinner about Atheism'. The reason for the choice of topic is obvious. It was the first opportunity to talk with their parents about cousin Bysshe's expulsion from Oxford. They were not hearing about it for the first time, however, as might perhaps be supposed. Five days earlier, while they were still at Bath, Charlotte had written on the back fly-leaf of her diary: 'April 2nd sorry to hear Bysshe was expelled Oxford for writing to the Bishops on Atheism'.

The expulsion of Shelley and Hogg took place on 25 March. News of it must have travelled swiftly to be known in Bath a week later. Interestingly, Charlotte makes no mention throughout the five weeks of her visit of any letter received from her parents or her brothers, but it is John or Charles who must appear the most likely source of the news: it was they who first knew what had happened. Shelley's first impulse, on leaving Oxford, had been to travel to London and make contact with his cousin John at Lincoln's Inn Fields, where Charles was also living. It was John who immediately took on the task of interceding with Shelley's father.

Shelley and Hogg, on their arrival in London, put up for the night at a coffee-house near Piccadilly. Having dined, they went to take tea with the Groves. Hogg was very much the odd man out and seems not to have realised that it was his presence which imposed a constraint on the conversation. His recollection, years later, is not a happy one:

> Here we passed a very silent evening; the cousins were taciturn people – the maxim of the family appeared to be, that a man should hold his tongue and save his money. I was a stranger; Bysshe (I heard him called by that name then for the first time; he was always called so by his family, probably to propitiate the old baronet) – Bysshe attempted to talk, but the cousins held their peace, and so conversation remained cousin-bound.[8]

Next day Shelley and Hogg found temporary lodgings in Poland Street and continued to visit Lincoln's Inn Fields for tea or dinner. One Sunday morning John Grove took them to Kensington Gardens, which became a favourite place for Shelley to visit.[9]

Normally, according to Charles Grove, Shelley and Hogg spent their mornings at Poland Street, engaged in writing. In the afternoons and evenings Charles was in their company, spending, he claimed, 'a part of every day with them'.[10] Two years younger than cousin Bysshe, and due that autumn to enter the college from which Hogg and Shelley had been expelled, Charles was evidently impressed and excited by the sophisticated Oxford aura of these unexpected companions. He spent 'many an afternoon and evening', he recalled, 'with Bysshe and Mr H at almost every coffee-house in London, for they changed their dining place daily for the sake of variety'.[11]

In fact, Hogg was in London for only three weeks, leaving Shelley to remain alone at Poland Street. Thrown by circumstances so closely into the company of his cousins, Shelley became interested in their medical studies. John Grove hoped to join the staff of St Bartholomew's Hospital. Charles had the desire to emulate his elder brother and, in addition to walking the wards, was attending a series of lectures by the celebrated Dr Abernethy. Their enthusiasm was infectious. Shelley responded to Charles's invitation to accompany him to the lectures and began to entertain the idea that his future also might lie in this direction. His intention to 'enter into the profession of physic', as he described it to Elizabeth Hitchener, persisted until the crisis of his elopement in August.[12]

Shelley's other form of companionship during the springtime weeks at Poland Street came from the Westbrooks. In his first letter to Hogg, after his friend's departure to Ellesmere in Shropshire, Shelley wrote, 'Miss Westbrooke has this moment called on me, with her sister. It certainly was very kind of her'.[13] Harriet Westbrook's elder sister, Eliza, played an important part in fostering Harriet's association with Shelley and he regarded her with much favour in the early stages. The age gap between the two sisters was considerable – fourteen years. It gave Eliza a particular value to Shelley as an impeccable chaperone for Harriet. In the following week, when Harriet had returned to her 'prison-house' – the school at Clapham – Shelley accompanied Eliza to the school and took Harriet out for a two-hour walk on Clapham Common. He was invited the following evening to dine with Eliza; her father would not be at home.[14]

Within days there came a dramatic development. Writing to Hogg from Lincoln's Inn Fields on 28 April, Shelley began, 'I am now at Grove's. I don't know where I am, where I will be. – Future present past is all a mist'. He had been drawn into the family tensions within the Westbrook's home as the result of an illness, or indisposition, affecting Harriet. He gave Hogg a graphic account of the part he had played:

My poor little friend has been ill, her sister sent for me the other night. I found her on a couch pale; – Her father is civil to me, very strangely, the sister is too civil by half. – she began talking about l'amour; I philosophised, & the youngest said she had such an headache that she could not bear conversation. – Her sister then went away, & I staid till ½ past 12. Her father had a large party below, he invited me – I refused. Yes! the fiend the wretch shall fall. Harriet will do for one of the crushers, & the eldest with some taming will do too. They are both very clever, & the youngest (my friend) is amiable. Yesterday she was better, today her father compelled her to go to Clapham, whither I have conducted her, & I am now returned.[15]

His increasing involvement with the Westbrooks became a running theme in subsequent letters to Hogg. 'I am now called to Miss [Eliza] Westbrook . . . I have been with her to Clapham . . . I spend most of my time at Miss Westbrooks . . . I am now at Miss Westbrooke's – she is reading Voltaire's Philosophique Dictionnaire . . . The Misses Westbrook are now very well' – these phrases occur in the final letters from London before Shelley's return to Sussex. And contact was to be maintained: 'I have arranged a correspondence with them', he wrote in his concluding paragraph. Once again he had hopes of recruiting female devotees to his coterie of 'the good, the disinterested, the free' who would accept his guidance in the crushing of the Christian fiend. Harriet was proving to be malleable; Eliza might require 'taming'.

The letters to Hogg form such a substantial part of our knowledge of Shelley at this time that they inevitably convey too narrow a view of him. The topics discussed with Hogg, and the attitudes adopted to them, are consonant with a *persona* invented by Shelley to suit this relationship. It is compounded of true self-awareness and fantasy, in a mode of high-mindedness which excludes altogether some of Shelley's other preoccupations and attributes. The Shelley presented to Hogg, and the Shelley recalled by his cousins, are by no means the same. When Charles Grove was Shelley's companion it was the lighter moods and high spirits of Shelley the prankster that were memorable. John Grove, for instance, recalled a farcical evening when Shelley and Charles went to a club in Covent Garden known as the British Forum:

> It was then a spouting club, in which Gale Jones and other Radicals abused all existing governments. Bysshe made so good a speech, complimenting and differing from the previous orators, that when he left the room, there was a rush to find out who he was, and to induce him to attend there again. He gave them a false name and address, not caring a farthing about the meeting, or the subjects there discussed.[16]

It was Charles who was most intimately in Shelley's confidence. He had accompanied Bysshe on the initial visit to the Westbrooks' house and would surely have known of the developing relationship with Harriet Westbrook. John Grove, nearly eight years older than Shelley, was more practically concerned in mediating between Mr Shelley and Bysshe. Mr Shelley made use of 49 Lincoln's Inn Fields as a convenient base when he was in London and there was at least one unplanned encounter there between father and son, when Shelley called one morning to see John Grove. 'I met my father in the passage', Shelley wrote, '& politely enquired after his health, he looked as black as a thunder cloud & said "Your most humble servant!" I made a low bow & wishing him a very good morning passed on'.[17]

John Grove did well to retain the goodwill of both father and son when their mutual antagonism was at its hottest. An immediate obstacle had been Shelley's loyalty to Hogg and determination to stand in solidarity with him. John Grove's strategy was to temporize until Hogg's father could arrange Hogg's departure from London, and then to look for some lessening of the more intransigent attitudes on both sides, which at present kept Shelley in exile from Field Place and without financial provision. It was in the evenhanded spirit of an intermediary that John Grove wrote to Timothy Shelley on 11 April 1811:

DEAR SIR, – Since I saw you I have had several conversations with Bysshe. I am convinced that there is nothing he wishes more than to be on terms with you and all his family, but he has got into his head ideas which he will not be prevailed on to relinquish till he is convinced of their being wrong, he is, however, very willing to be put right. I have told him he ought to consider that your and Mrs Shelley's happiness depend on his conduct, that he ought not to sacrifice everything to his own opinions and be entirely regardless of your feelings, and bid him think what a wretched life he must lead if he forced you to withdraw your support and affection from him, which I assured him you would do if he did not agree to your proposals. Mr Hogg's father is now in Town and I believe at this minute talking with him, I think if he takes his son out of Town you will find Bysshe inclined to agree to most of your proposals, if not to all. Bysshe considers himself at present bound by honour to remain with Hogg until he is reconciled to his father, if that recollection should take place this evening I have great hopes that he would then think of nothing but returning to his duty. I fully intended to have called on you this morning but was prevented by want of time. Bysshe expressed a great wish this morning to go to Field Place but yet he would not prevail on himself to accede to all your terms. His opinions I think may in time be changed; he appears to me to be waivering already. I beg to be remembered to Mrs Shelley and Elizabeth. – I remain, Yours sincerely,

JOHN GROVE[18]

To play for time and a cooling of tempers was John's policy and it sustained him as the channel of informal negotiation. About a fortnight later, Mr Shelley was again in London, 'as fierce as a lion', and there was a fresh discussion during which, in Shelley's account:

John Grove saw him, succeeded in flattering him into a promise that he wd. allow me 200£ [*sic*] per an., & leave me to misery. Now he has left town, & written to disan[n]ul all that

he before promised. Nemus [Latin for *Grove*] is flattering like a
courtier, & will I conjecture bring him about again.[19]

Another Grove brother who appeared in London during April
and was drawn into consideration of Shelley's difficulties was the
eldest, Tom, who brought his wife to spend a few weeks in town.
Because of the disparity in their ages, and his married status, Tom
would have had very little previous acquaintance with cousin
Bysshe, but he was evidently charmed by him. He and Henrietta
intended to go to their estate in Wales, Cwm Elan, in the summer
and invited Bysshe to join them there for a period of tranquillity and
recuperation after the stormy events of recent weeks. It was a
considerate offer, of which he availed himself.

Shelley would doubtless have heard previously of Cwm Elan as a
happy memory of cousin Harriet's childhood. Now in April 1811, in
the frequent company of three of her brothers, he could hardly fail
to think of her sometimes, though I have no doubt that it was the
other Harriet, the youngest Miss Westbrook, who commanded his
attention. There is, however, a suggestion that while Shelley was in
London he received a letter from Harriet Grove. This turns, once
again, on the interpretation of Shelley's use of 'she' and 'her' in a
letter to Hogg. In his edition of Shelley's letters, Frederick Jones
added a footnote, in 1964, to the letter (No. 62) of 26 April 1811 to
Hogg, making the cautious comment that 'It would seem that
Shelley had actually had a letter from Harriet [Grove] explaining
why she would not and could not continue their correspondence,
and making it clear that she was not yet married'.

The justification for this occurs in a passage towards the end of
one of the longest letters, which is devoted mainly to handling a
mood of despair in Hogg and rehearsing the familiar arguments
against Christianity. Much of it is in Shelley's more cryptic and
sibylline manner until, as in previous instances, there comes a
sudden outburst which has no apparent connection with what
precedes it:

> She is <u>not</u> lost for ever – how I hope that may be true, but I fear
> <u>I</u> can never ascertain, <u>I</u> can never influence an amelioration,
> as she does not any longer permit an <u>Atheist</u> to correspond

with her. She talks of Duty to her Father. And this is your Religion.[20]

It is my view that Shelley is here referring, not to Harriet Grove, but to his sister Elizabeth. Indeed the whole letter seems to be coloured by Hogg's despair over his rejection by Elizabeth and his hope that she may not be lost for ever. Shelley seems to me to be picking up the phrase from Hogg's letter – 'not lost for ever' – and adding his own hopeful comment, but with the caution that he himself can no longer influence Elizabeth.

I propose this with confidence because a subsequent letter to Hogg makes it clear that Shelley had been shattered to learn that, of all his expected supporters, Elizabeth – at one time the staunchest of all – had defected to their father's side. In an unequivocal reference to Elizabeth, Shelley wrote:

> My Sister does not come to Town, nor will she ever at least I can see no chance of it. I will not deceive you, she is lost, lost to everything, Xtianity has tainted her, she talks of God & Xt – I would not venture thus to prophesy without being most perfectly convinced in my own mind of the truth of what I say.[21]

The notion of Harriet writing to reassure Shelley that she was not married is quite preposterous. She was not privy, as we are, to his correspondence with Hogg and had no reason to think that Shelley could believe her to be married – least of all when he was in daily contact with her brothers, who could instantly disabuse him. As to a resumption of their letter-writing to each other, there is nothing more than the dubious evidence cited above to suggest that this could any longer be an issue. Harriet Grove may have been the 'she' who was 'lost for ever' at Christmas 1810, but by April 1811 Elizabeth Shelley was the lost one. Half a year had passed since Shelley last had a letter from Harriet: and half a year is a long time in the calendar of teenage romance.

· *Chapter Nine* ·

The entry in Charlotte Grove's diary for 12 May 1811 reads, 'Harriet & myself walked after dinner for the first time this spring. Bysshe Shelley is returned home'. The news had travelled swiftly. Shelley left London on 10 May and went first to Nelson Hall, the appropriately named home of his uncle, Captain John Pilfold, RN, at Lindfield, near Cuckfield; he did not arrive at Field Place until the 13th. A settlement of the differences with his father had been achieved, by which Shelley was to have an income of £200 per annum and the liberty to live where he pleased. In so far as he was capable of planning ahead, Shelley hoped that within a year he and Hogg would set up a joint residence in London, where Hogg could study law and Shelley surgery. Meanwhile, Hogg was settled for the time being at York and Shelley was restored to the domestic company of his mother and sisters – separation from whom had been a genuine hardship.[1]

He found Elizabeth just recovering from scarlet fever. He was able to assure Hogg that she was now restored physically, though not in her mental state[2] – with which one can only sympathise, since she was torn by conflicting loyalties to her father and brother, and pestered with the amorous advances of the egregious Hogg. Shelley, who was not one to accept frustrations patiently, had to realise that he no longer enjoyed his old philosophical mastery over her, and that his dream of uniting her in a love match with Hogg had become a nightmare. She had 'murdered thought', he wrote; he mourned her 'as no more', considering her as dead.[3]

This loss of his prime acolyte threw Shelley into a dangerous mood. Harriet Westbrook was inaccessible during the term in school – 'in prison', as Shelley preferred to call it. He probably became bored and restless at Field Place without the stimulus that Elizabeth usually gave him. He had no other congenial female company, so he resorted to the familiar practice of correspondence with a talented young woman to whom he was a stranger. His choice this time was Janetta Phillips,[4] some of whose poems Shelley had read in a manuscript shown to him by a Mr Strong, who took fright at Shelley's expulsion from Oxford and broke off their contact. Shelley therefore took the liberty of writing directly to Miss Phillips, describing himself as 'an enthusiastic adorer of genius' who was prepared to have her poems published at his expense. Having made this tempting offer he then trailed his coat on 'the speculative points of religion' and awaited a reply. Miss Phillips's reply has not survived, but Shelley confessed that he was 'surprised, extremely surprised' by it. His offer was rejected. Later in the year her poems were published by an Oxford printer by subscription. Among the subscribers was Shelley, who took fifteen copies, of which three went to Lincoln's Inn Fields for the Groves.[5]

A not dissimilar venture, but with vastly greater consequences, sprang from a casual visit to Uncle John at Nelson Hall, where he met a schoolmistress whose pupils included one of Captain Pilfold's daughters. The schoolmistress was Elizabeth Hitchener, of about the same age as Eliza Westbrook and making a similar appeal to Shelley as a possible recruit to his intimate female circle. Without delay he directed suitable books into her hands and began a correspondence which progressively exalted her to the status of Sister of his Soul before she ultimately and inevitably declined to the 'Brown Demon' of their final phase and was dismissed by him as 'an artful, superficial, ugly, hermaphroditical beast of a woman' – as he described her to Hogg.[6]

While Shelley remained in Sussex through May and June 1811 there was little contact with his cousins. John Grove and Charles apparently stayed in London, where they were able, by the influence of the Duchess of Rutland, to visit Carlton House. Of the seafaring brothers, William and George, the only news was that William was now a first lieutenant on the frigate *Hecate*, preparing to seize the island of Java. Tom Grove and his wife Henrietta were at their Dorset home, near Blandford, while at Tollard Royal the two sisters, Harriet and Charlotte, were greatly dependent on each other's company. They kept themselves awake at night 'building Welsh castles' – a favourite activity of Charlotte's. By day they found entertainment in their own high spirits. 'Amused ourselves in packing up the box of books & also in some indescribable mischief known only to Harriet & myself', Charlotte wrote in her diary. In a subsequent entry, 'We walked out in the evening and played our flageolets to the cows whilst they were milked. My father saw us & laughed at us'. On 25 June she noted, 'Harriet & myself walked in the hayfield. She <u>impudently</u> threw me on the haycocks'.[7] The following day was Harriet's twentieth birthday.

Before the end of June Tom Grove was preparing to make the journey into Wales where he and Henrietta would spend the summer months at his estate, Cwm Elan. The earlier invitation to Shelley to join them there had now to be given practical form and the necessary arrangements made for his arrival at the beginning of July, when the London coach would set him down at Rhayader. It may of course have been the merest coincidence that the Westbrooks also planned to visit Wales at this time, but it would not have escaped Shelley's notice that at their destination, Aberystwyth, they would be little more than thirty miles away. When he arrived at Rhayader, in what was then Radnorshire, he already had an understanding that Eliza and Harriet Westbrook would shortly 'proceed to Aberystwyth where I shall meet them'.[8] Meanwhile he was to stay on the outskirts of Rhayader, at Cwm Elan.

The estate, purchased in 1792 by Thomas Grove senior, comprised '10,999 almost worthless acres', which, according to a contemporary account, 'the new proprietor is now converting into a paradise'. Mr Grove had erected a 'neat and elegant mansion' and employed a manager to operate a lead-mine in the valley of the Elan.[9] The ruined buildings of the mine survive but the mansion has long been submerged in a vast reservoir from which the city of Birmingham draws its water supply.

What attracted Thomas Grove to Radnorshire is not clear, but it may be significant that the county's High Sheriff in 1784 was Shelley's grandfather, Bysshe Shelley, whose son Timothy became Grove's brother-in-law in 1791 by marrying Elizabeth Pilfold. It may therefore have been the Shelleys, with their first-hand knowledge of Radnorshire, who aroused Thomas Grove's interest in Cwm Elan in 1792. In 1807 it was Mr Grove who became High Sheriff for the county, and his son Tom followed him in that office in 1809, 1812 and 1813.

Shelley was not the first poet to visit the Groves at Cwm Elan and commemorate their estate in verse. That distinction goes to William Lisle Bowles, whose sonnets made so deep an impression on Coleridge that he visited Donhead St Andrew in order to meet Bowles and express his admiration. As curate at Donhead, Bowles had an easy intimacy with the Groves at Ferne and was invited to Cwm Elan in the mid-1790s. His poem 'Coombe-Ellen', published in 1798 and inscribed to Thomas Grove, begins with an invocation to the spirit of wild untamed Nature in the Romantic style that Shelley inherited and developed:

> Call the strange spirit that abides unseen
> In wilds, and wastes, and shaggy solitudes,
> And bid his dim hand lead thee through these scenes
> That burst immense around! By mountains, glens,
> And solitary cataracts that dash
> Through dark ravines.

Among the legendary and historical themes suggested by this inspiring landscape there are vividly sketched vignettes of scenes easily recognisable by their directness and simplicity:

> No sound is here,
> Save of the stream that shrills, and now and then
> A cry as of faint wailing, when the kite
> Comes sailing o'er the crags, or straggling lamb
> Bleats for its mother.

The poem reaches its climax when the poet ends his contemplation of the awesome solitude and pristine beauty of untouched Nature with the thought that human cultivation can further enhance the scene:

> here I bid farewell
> To Fancy's fading pictures, and farewell
> The ideal spirit that abides unseen
> 'Mid rocks, and woods and solitudes. I hail
> Rather the steps of Culture, that ascend

The precipice's side. She bids the wild
Bloom, and adorns with beauty not its own
The ridged mountain's tract; she speaks, and lo!
The yellow harvest nods upon the slope;
And through the dark and matted moss upshoots
The bursting clover, smiling to the sun.
These are thy offspring, Culture![10]

Whether or not they were appropriate to the terrain, Grove evidently introduced the new arable rotation and clover seeding-mixtures that were favoured by the agricultural innovators in Wiltshire. Reclamation and improvement of heath, moor and upland were undertaken with great fervour at the end of the eighteenth century, but this was not an aspect of Cwm Elan that interested Shelley. In comparison with Bowles, his approach is deeply introspective. His invocation of Bowles's 'strange spirit that abides unseen' conjures up a dark raven-like spirit, macabre in the Gothic manner, a 'thing of gloom':

Dark Spirit of the desart rude
That o'er this awful solitude,
Each tangled and untrodden wood,
Each dark and silent glen below,
Where sunlight's gleamings never glow,
Whilst jetty, musical and still,
In darkness speeds the mountain rill;
That o'er yon broken peaks sublime,
Wild shapes that mock the scythe of time,
And the pure Ellan's foamy course,
Wavest thy wand of magic force;
Art thou yon sooty and fearful fowl
That flaps its wing o'er the leafless oak
That o'er the dismal scene doth scowl
And mocketh music with its croak?[11]

The letters he wrote from Cwm Elan show that Shelley was evidently impressed, as he could hardly fail to be, by the scenic beauty of his surroundings – 'rocks piled on each other to tremendous heights, rivers formed into cataracts by their projections, & valleys clothed with woods',[12] as he described them to Elizabeth Hitchener. To Graham he adopted a more facetious tone: 'This is a most delightful place but more adapted for the Rosa-Matildan than the Petrio-Pindaric style of raphsodizing [sic]. Here are rocks, cataracts, woods & Groves.'[13]

In the general tumult of his feelings at this time Shelley was not in the mood for quiet contemplation of the beauties of Nature, no matter how picturesque and romantic they might be. 'This is most divine scenery', he wrote to Hogg, 'but all very dull stale flat & unprofitable – indeed this place is a very great bore'.[14] That first impression was modified later – 'I am more astonished at the grandeur of this scenery than I expected'; but he added 'I do not now much regard it. I have other things to think of'.[15]

Among those other things was a tangle of unfulfilled intentions to be justified or explained away. When Shelley left Field Place his first destination was London where he was to stay for some days, presumably at Lincoln's Inn Fields, since Hogg wrote to him care of John Grove. Elizabeth Hitchener, who was in London, expected Shelley to call on her. Hogg, at York, believed that the coach which carried his friend out of London would be bound for York, not for Wales. The appeasement of his disappointed correspondents was one of the first tasks for Shelley when Tom Grove and Henrietta welcomed him as their guest.

To Elizabeth Hitchener he pleaded 'a short but violent nervous illness', but for which 'nothing else could have prevented my calling on you in town'.[16] As it is not mentioned to Hogg or any other correspondent, this illness sounds suspiciously like the tactical variety which occurs providentially when an alibi is needed. It was occasioned by 'several nights of sleeplessness and days of pressing & urgent business'. It is difficult to identify the nature of the business which 'would neither admit of delay or rest', unless one harbours the thought that it involved time spent with the Westbrooks. 'Well,' Shelley added rather lamely, 'here I now am'. He resigned himself to the postponement of the pleasure of Miss Hitchener's conversation.

To Hogg Shelley protested, 'You did me injustice by supposing that my own will detained me from York'. The reason was lack of money. 'I have at this moment no money,' he wrote to Hogg. 'You will see me when I can get some'. Again, three days later, 'It is my intention as soon as financial strength will permit me to evacuate these solitudes to come to York'. And once more, at the end of July, 'I am <u>here</u> for the present absolutely because I have no money to come to York'. Hogg's response was to send another £10 to add to the £20 he had already provided. He was clearly aware of Shelley's growing involvement with Harriet Westbrook and teased him about it, but Shelley was not to be drawn. 'Yr. jokes on H. Westbrook amuse me', he retorted. 'It is a common error for people to fancy others' in their situation but if I know anything about <u>Love</u> I am <u>not</u> in love. I have heard from the Westbrooks, both of whom I esteem'.[17]

Shelley's inner confusion while he was at Cwm Elan is understandable. He wanted to be reunited with Hogg. His emotionally charged involvements with Elizabeth Hitchener and the West-brooks were increasing their pressure. He still held the belief that his future career would be in surgery but in the immediate present he had no money and no clear plan.[18] His extended stay at Cwm Elan was tolerable only in default of any better alternative. There was no meeting of minds with Tom Grove. Writing to Elizabeth Hitchener Shelley commented, 'I am now with people who, strange to say, never <u>think</u>'.[19] To Hogg he expressed himself in similar terms: 'I am all solitude, as I cannot call the society here an alternative to it'.[20]

Certainly the radical style of thinking in which Shelley was engaged would not have touched an answering chord in Tom Grove, who seems to have been conventional in his outlook and rather snobbish in the cultivation of his friendships with noble lords and their noble ladies. 'How many dukes shall we have today?' had been a joke between John Grove and Shelley when they went to dine with Tom in their London days together.[21] As the eldest of the brothers, Tom was nine years older than his cousin, who was just approaching his nineteenth birthday – a large enough interval at that age to emphasise the difference in their allegiances.

It seems unlikely, therefore, that Shelley found any relief in unburdening himself to Tom, but with Charles Grove the case was otherwise. Shelley maintained contact with Charles by letters which unfortunately have not survived, though one from Cwm Elan was summarised by Charles in his later memoirs. The news it conveyed was startling. It announced that Shelley felt he had received a summons 'to link his fate with another'. His mood was in the melodramatic vein of much of his writing: the letter ended with the words, 'Hear it not, Percy, for it is a knell, which summons thee to heaven or to hell!'[22]

The identity of the other person with whom Shelley now contemplated linking his fate would have come as no surprise to Charles Grove, who was in Shelley's confidence at this time. The precipitate nature of the decision could hardly have been foreseen, however, even by Hogg whose teasing suspicion was confirmed so suddenly and abruptly by Shelley's announcement: 'I shall certainly come to York, but Harriet Westbrook will decide whether now or in 3 weeks'. By way of explanation his letter continued:

Her father has persecuted her in a most horrible way, & endeavours to compel her to go to school. She asked my advice: resistance was the answer at the same time that I essayed to mollify old W[estbrook] in vain! & in consequence of my advice she has thrown herself upon my protection! I set off for London on Monday [August 5]. How flattering a distinction: – I am thinking of ten million things at once. What have I said I declare quite ludicrous – I advised her to resist – she wrote to say that resistance was useless, but that she would fly with me, & threw herself on my protection. – We shall have 200£ [*sic*] a year, when we find it run short we must live I suppose upon love. Gratitude & admiration all demand that I should love her forever.[23]

In London Shelley used Edward Graham's Sackville Street address as a *pied à terre* and also made use of 49 Lincoln's Inn Fields in the customary way. In his first letter to Hogg after leaving Cwm Elan he wrote, 'I am now dining at John Grove's.'[24] Here he learned from Charles Grove that John was actively courting Shelley's sister Elizabeth. Next day Shelley took the coach to Horsham to hear Elizabeth's views, returning at once to London, from where he wrote to inform Hogg that Elizabeth 'appeared rather chagrined at the intelligence: she fears that she will lose an entertaining acquaintance who sometimes enlivens her solitude, by his conversion into a more serious character of a lover. I do not think she will, as his attachment is that of a cool unimpassioned selector of a companion for life'.[25]

With this reassurance to Hogg, Shelley combined a warning that Elizabeth's rejection of John Grove meant no 'augmented leniency' for Hogg; and he went on to regret that he had ever mentioned Elizabeth's name to Hogg, whom he urged to forget her. The nature of Shelley's opposition to a marriage uniting his sister with Harriet Grove's brother is sufficiently complex to foster a variety of interpretations. His assessment of John as 'a cool unimpassioned selector of a companion for life' is probably just and would be equally true of most of his contemporaries. As a lover John evidently lacked some essential talent. Charlotte's matchmaking notes in her diaries recorded his disappointments. Later in the same year there were hopes of success with another cousin, Flora Long. 'John & Miss Flora jumped over the stiles very prettily together', Charlotte wrote, on 29 September 1811, adding 'Good luck attend JG in Cupid's court'.[26] But her brother's luck was out, as it was to be again in 1813 in his courtship of Miss Eyre of Newhouse. Charlotte's account is dramatic in its succinctness:

Jan 1. John received a New Year's gift from Miss Eyre.

Jan 2. We are invited to New House. Things put on a promising appearance.

Jan 9. My father went to Newhouse.

Jan 11. I & my brother went to Newhouse, called at Netherhampton for John on our way.

Jan 20. We went to Newhouse. The old Eyre gave us a cool reception. Mr Popham there.

Jan 21. A thunderbolt upon us all. John looked the picture of woe. Mr Popham went home. The old lady went to bed with a headache.

Jan 22. We took a hasty flight from Newhouse. Went to Netherhampton, my aunts & us talked over the behaviour of a certain lady.

Jan 23. My father planned a nice scheme. Miss Kneller to be Cupid's messenger.

Jan 24. I received a note which looks favorable.

Jan 26. John rode over to Salisbury but was disappointed in

meeting with Miss Eyre. Miss Kneller is very strenuous in the cause. My father wrote to Mr Popham on this subject.

Jan 27. John wrote a letter to Miss Eyre.

Jan 29. A letter from Mr Popham. He has given my father's letter to Miss Eyre but he cannot interfere any further in this business.

Jan 31. [An entry beginning 'Miss Eyre' has been heavily deleted. All that remains is as follows] John called on Aunt Jackson. My brother, I hope, will soon get over it.[27]

He was in no hurry to make a fresh attempt. Four years were to pass before John married, taking as his wife one of the many daughters of Sir William Fraser, whose wife – *née* Betty Farquharson – was a half-sister of Tom Grove's wife Henrietta. In his search for a suitable and congenial 'companion for life', John Grove tended to look among his kinsfolk and landed neighbours – a very different style from cousin Bysshe's.

In August 1811 Harriet Westbrook seems to have been unnerved by the consequence of her impulsive appeal to Shelley. His immediate return to London and evident readiness to take her under his protection imposed on her a greater pressure than she had perhaps anticipated. For a sixteen-year-old girl to elope, with no pledge or guarantee of marriage, was a daunting step to take. The August days slipped by while she remained undecided and Shelley's resolve strengthened. He visited her several times, with Charles Grove as his companion, before she made up her mind. Early one morning Charles and Shelley in a hackney coach picked her up and drove to the inn in the City where they waited until the northern mail coach was ready to depart. Charles stayed with them as their only supporter, to wave farewell when the coach set out on the road to York. After their departure he had one last service to perform – to post to Mr Shelley the letter that Bysshe had entrusted to him. It was an ironical conclusion to the might-have-been romance of that other Harriet, Charles's sister.[28]

A few days later Charles left London to travel home with his brother John, going first to see the new mansion at Ferne which was nearly completed. He can hardly have withheld some account of Bysshe's elopement with Miss Westbrook, but there is no reference to it in Charlotte's diary. The two topics that occupied her attention were the imminent removal from Tollard Royal to the newly rebuilt home at Ferne and the nightly spectacle of a comet. According to the *Gentleman's Magazine*, this comet, 'which makes so brilliant an appearance', was first observed in southern France in the spring but did not add its novelty to English skies until late August or early September. Charlotte first mentions it on 6 September.[29] Three days later Charles had managed to convince himself that there were two comets.

If comets are to be regarded as portents of some stirring event, Charlotte might have noticed that 6 September was also the first occasion when she and Harriet met William Helyar since their chance encounter five months earlier while they were driving back from Bath and passed through Sedgehill. This new meeting was also unplanned. 'Met Mr J. & W. Helyar on our way to Fern' is Charlotte's brief note. It was the prelude, however, to some unmistakable planning in which her brothers seem to have taken the initiative. On 9 September John invited William Helyar to shoot with him and dine with the family afterwards. They all walked up the hill after tea to look at the comet.

The immediate preoccupation during the rest of September was the packing up at Tollard Royal and the removal of the Grove household to Ferne. 'Waggons going off', Charlotte wrote. 'Bustle & confusion'. Going down Ashcombe Hill one of the wagons overturned. After three nights under their new roof the Groves went off to Chippenham races, staying with their Long kinsfolk nearby. They returned to Ferne on 30 September, the day before John and Charles were due to go to Sedgehill for a day's shooting with William Helyar. The two brothers stayed overnight at Sedgehill and brought William back with them next day to Ferne, where Tom Grove joined them. It is not difficult to imagine that the shooting party at Sedgehill had provided the opportunity to discuss an alliance of the two families, if William wished to propose and Harriet were disposed to accept.

It was put to the test immediately. Helyar stayed through the day and danced with Harriet in the evening. Charlotte confided in her diary, 'I have hopes that what I wish may happen'. Next day, 3 October, she was able to confirm her hopes: 'Our castles have a good foundation. Harriet checkmated by WH'.[30] In the afternoon Helyar took his future wife out for a drive in his curricle and again they danced in the evening. In the following days he went to Coker Court, the family seat of the Helyars, to discuss the marriage arrangements with his parents; and on his return he took Harriet and Charlotte to Sedgehill to inspect Harriet's future home. The Groves made social visits to neighbouring grandees – the Arundells at Wardour and the Wyndhams at Dinton – to be congratulated on Harriet's engagement; and on 21 October the family coach set off from Ferne to London, with William Helyar in the party. Their first day's journey took them as far as Halford Bridge where they spent the night, and Charlotte wrote in her diary, 'Harriet & I read to Mr Wm. Helyar all the way'. Their father and brothers met them next day at Hounslow. At 49 Lincoln's Inn Fields they were joined in the evening by 'my uncle', as Charlotte recorded, who 'told us odd circumstances'.

There can be no doubt that the uncle was Captain John Pilfold, who had that day accompanied Bysshe Shelley to London from Cuckfield. The circumstances that he was able to disclose were indeed *odd*. On the previous day he had received the following letter from Timothy Shelley:

> Mr Shelley understands his son is with Captain Pilfold. Mr S. begs to apprise Captain P. that his son's irrational notions, and the absence of all sentiment of Duty and affection, and the unusual spirit of Resistance to any control has determined Mr S. not to admit him, but to place everything respecting him into the hands of Mr Whitton, that no other person may interfere.[31]

Feelings were running so high that Mr Shelley was convinced the household at Field Place was in danger of some sort of riotous intrusion by Bysshe, if he were allowed to return from Cuckfield. To his lawyer, Whitton, he wrote, 'He frightened his mother and sister exceedingly, and now if they hear a Dog Bark they run upstairs'.[32] For his personal protection, Mr Shelley was prepared to swear in Especial Constables around himself.

While Bysshe was his uncle's guest at Cuckfield he wrote to Tom Medwin's father at Horsham, asking him to act on his behalf in preparing a marriage settlement.[33] In their flight, Shelley and

Harriet Westbrook had gone on from York to Edinburgh, where they went through a form of marriage under Scottish law. It was Shelley's intention to marry her in England subsequently.* For the moment she remained in York, to be rejoined by Shelley after his brief sortie into Sussex on family business. He had travelled to London with Uncle John as the first stage of his return journey northward.

For Shelley to have united himself in this headstrong way with the daughter of a coffee-house proprietor – even a relatively affluent one – was a social disaster and a culpable folly in the eyes of his father and his grandfather. The staunch support of John Pilfold was all the more valuable at such a time. It emphasised his unusual role as a paternal figure who in some measure filled the gap left by Timothy Shelley's withdrawal of fatherly affection, and added to the friction between the two older men which has been noted earlier.

Now, having imparted the 'odd circumstances' to the Groves at Lincoln's Inn Fields, Captain John went about his own business and they settled down to a few days spent in shopping, socialising and theatre-going. They visited the Lyceum and Covent Garden, saw Mrs Siddons and Kemble acting, and William treated the sisters to that tasty novelty, ice. There were items to be selected for Harriet's trousseau, in London and also locally when they returned to Ferne. 'Harriet measured for <u>Fatimas</u>', Charlotte noted. 'Wishes to have them large enough: provident certainly'.

Charles Grove would have been particularly interested in Uncle John's account of recent events in Sussex, as he was continuing to correspond with Bysshe and trying to help him. He may even have had a brief meeting with him during the few hours Bysshe spent in London before making his connection with the coach to York. Either then, or by letter, he suggested to his cousin that the Duke of Norfolk, who was the political patron of the Shelleys, might be persuaded to intervene and pacify Mr Shelley.

Writing to Charles a week later, Shelley thanked him for this advice, saying he had availed himself of it, had written to the Duke and expected 'the most salutary effects'. He also asked Charles for any fresh news of events at Field Place and commented that Captain

---

* He did so, though not until 24 March 1814.

John Pilfold 'has behaved nobly to us'. The general tone of the letter indicates the confidence he placed in Charles. In particular he valued Charles's loyalty and discretion: 'You do not shew my letters'. As for himself, he was surprisingly sanguine: 'I expect that all things will go well. I depend on your promises as does Harriet, who has desired me to send her best love to you, to welcome you to us whenever circumstances permit'.[34]

With the knowledge that William Helyar had been visiting Lincoln's Inn Fields with Harriet Grove, Shelley asked Charles, 'How do you like Mr Helyar, a new brother as well as a new cousin must be an invaluable acquisition'. In a postscript he wrote, 'Tell John I am happy to find we are as good friends as ever. . . . Remember me to him, & all the family'.

In his earlier letter Charles must have reminded Shelley that some of his books remained at 49 Lincoln's Inn Fields and would be sent to him if he needed them. Shelley's answer was, 'Let my books sleep in peace until more time'.[35] I believe they slept on there until they were gathered up with the other contents of the house and removed to Wiltshire. If that is the case, one of them was the pocket book and daily journal that Shelley had used in 1809. In the pocket at the back was a carefully wrapped lock of hair. On the paper enfolding it were the initials H.G.

A fortnight later Harriet Grove married William Helyar.[36]

· Chapter Ten ·

The general course of Shelley's life from 1812 onwards lies outside my scope, which is confined to the family relationships that linked Field Place and Ferne. Shelley's marriage, followed by Harriet Grove's, weakened those links, but there were other factors as well. The house in Lincoln's Inn Fields, which had had a pivotal importance as meeting-place and staging post, was no longer regularly occupied by John and Charles. During 1812 Charles was at Oxford during terms and at Ferne in the vacations; his interest in medicine was lapsing as his thoughts turned towards ordination and a future as a country parson. John is not mentioned in Charlotte's diary throughout the first eight months of 1812 and it may be that it was in this period he resided in Edinburgh to pursue his medical studies there. He reappeared at Ferne in September and was based at home until the following February, engaged mainly in his courtship of the perfidious Miss Eyre.

As for Shelley, his movements were carrying him further away from the familiar scenes of London and Sussex. After his return to York from Cuckfield in October 1811 he moved to the Lake District with his wife and her sister Eliza, renting a cottage at Keswick and making the acquaintance of Robert Southey. In February they sailed to Ireland and remained there until April. If Shelley maintained any lingering contact with his Wiltshire cousins it must have been in correspondence with Charles; and for that there is some evidence, although it is of a less than satisfactory nature.

In her diary entry for 19 December 1811, Charlotte wrote, 'Charles arrived ... entertained us with his account of Bysshe Shelley'. The obvious inference is that he had something fresh to add to the 'odd circumstances' recounted by Uncle John Pilfold to the family circle in London on 22 October. Charlotte had been among

those present then and must be presumed therefore to have learned
that Shelley had been denied admittance to Field Place and had
travelled to London with their uncle *en route* to York where his newly
wed wife was waiting to be reunited with him. It is difficult to
imagine that, two months later, Charles could have had anything
new to add. He had received from Bysshe the letter quoted at the
end of the previous chapter, but its relaxed and almost bland tone
could scarcely be less 'entertaining' in the telling and gives no
indication of the emotional turbulence that engulfed Shelley on his
arrival at York and breached his friendship with Hogg. Charlotte's
choice of the word 'entertained' suggests that Charles was drawing
on a direct experience of some kind or had received some further
communication from Shelley. It is of course possible, but most
unlikely, that during November Charles might have elected to go to
Keswick, fortified by the message of welcome in Shelley's letter.
Conversely, Shelley's movements at the time are well documented
and there is no reason to suppose that he could have journeyed
south to any place where Charles might have met him.

Within the remaining limits of probability two guesses are
plausible. One is that Charles entertained the family with a minute-
by-minute account of his part in Shelley's initial elopement with
Harriet Westbrook in August, though he might be expected to have
done this already. The alternative is that he had received a lively and
entertaining account of the Shelleys' visit to a house party at
Greystoke, near Penrith, as the guests of the Duke of Norfolk,
during the first week of December.[1] It will be remembered that
Charles had urged Bysshe to make an approach to the Duke as a
likely mediator with Timothy Shelley, and it was indeed the Duke
who eventually fostered a measure of peace between Bysshe and his
father. Bysshe was certainly pleased with the agreeable nature of
the visit to Greystoke and it would be no surprise if he sent Charles
a detailed and graphic account of the event.

More difficult, if not downright impossible to interpret, is
Charles's statement, in his letter of 16 February 1857, to Hellen
Shelley:

The following spring [i.e. 1812] I saw Bysshe and Mrs Shelley
in London. They spent the summer of that year, 1812, with my

brother and sister at Cwm Elan. Mrs G. was very much pleased with Mrs Shelley, and sorry when they left them. They intended at that time to settle in Wales, but I think they went to the Lakes instead, Bysshe having become acquainted with Southey. From that time I never saw Bysshe again. My brother [John] may have seen something of him, either in town, or in Edinburgh, but I do not quite recollect how that was.[2]

Shelley's second visit to Cwm Elan, in the summer of 1812, is well substantiated, but it is difficult to see how Charles could have met Bysshe and his wife in London in the spring. During March the Shelleys were in Ireland. They landed at Holyhead on 6 April with the intention of looking for a suitable home in Wales. Eight days later they were in the vicinity of Rhayader, inspecting and temporarily occupying the farm at Nantgwillt for which they hoped to acquire a lease. Here they remained while negotiations proceeded, involving Captain Pilfold and Mr Medwin as the potential backers of the financial transaction which would enable Shelley to establish his ideal commune. To Harriet Shelley and her sister would be added Elizabeth Hitchener as soon as she could break away from her home circle in Sussex. There were thoughts of a journey by Shelley and Harriet to liberate her and escort her back to Wales, but this did not materialise. Money was scarce and had to be husbanded. In the circumstances it seems improbable that the Shelleys would have passed through London during the spring. There is certainly no record, so far as I am aware, that such a long and costly journey from Rhayader was undertaken. Charles, incidentally, on the evidence of Charlotte's diary, spent the Easter vacation at Ferne and returned to Oxford on 10 April.

In considering the testimony of Charles Grove it must always be remembered that he was trying to bridge a gap of nearly fifty years. It is hardly surprising, therefore, if he sometimes assigns an event to the wrong year. His sugggestion that, in the autumn of 1812, the Shelleys were in the Lake District making the acquaintance of Robert Southey is a case in point. This episode belongs to 1811, not 1812. Similarly, his meeting with Bysshe and Harriet in London – so very unlikely in the spring of 1812, where he places it – could easily have taken place in the autumn of that year, when they were certainly in London.

The summertime sojourn at Cwm Elan fits Charles's account, though it was briefer and rather more impromptu than he implies. Shelley's intention was to establish a permanent occupancy of the Nantgwillt farm during the summer and to meet his cousin Tom as a neighbour, not, as in 1811, as his host. Surprisingly he does not seem to have looked to Tom Grove for any help with the negotiations for the lease of the farm, though when the need arose for a valuation of the contents he informed Medwin that 'Mr T. Grove has kindly promised to find a proper person to stand on my side'.[3]

However, it was the two Sussex gentlemen, Captain Pilfold and Mr Medwin, who acted in Shelley's interest over the lease, scrutinised the small print of the proposition, foresaw danger and withdrew. At the end of the first week in June the Shelleys were obliged to quit the farm. It was as refugees from sudden homelessness that they turned to cousin Tom and Henrietta.

The disappointment of Harriet Shelley is easy to imagine. Since her elopement she had lived in temporary lodgings in Scotland, the north of England and Ireland: the prospect of a settled home in what she described as 'an old family house, with a farm of 200 acres meadow land' where 'Percy's little circle' could settle down to practise his ideals of community life, must have been immensely appealing. To have it snatched away, for lack of money, was a grievous blow made no easier to bear by being thrust into the company of Percy's high-living relatives, with whom she could have little in common. According to Charles Grove, his sister-in-law Henrietta 'was very much pleased with Mrs Shelley' and there seems to have been a degree of mutual rapport between the two women, but a letter of Harriet's to a friend, written at Cwm Elan on 7 June, indicates the strain inherent in the situation: 'Percy is related to Mr Grove, and his wife is a very pleasant woman, tho' too formal to be agreeable. He is a very proud man. Therefore you may guess how we pass our time.'[4] About a fortnight passed in this manner before the Shelleys moved on to a fruitless exploration of Chepstow, followed by a journey westward along the English coast of the

Bristol Channel as far as Lynmouth, which became the next of their temporary homes.

Thereafter Shelley had little contact with any of his Wiltshire cousins. No trace of a continuing correspondence with Charles Henry Grove has survived. John maintained a readiness to act as an intermediary between Shelley and Sir Timothy, but to little effect. In May 1813 Shelley's wife, who was pregnant, had hopes of a reconciliation that would admit her and Bysshe to Field Place – hopes that were aroused by a renewed contact with John Grove. Writing from London to her friend, Mrs Nugent, she recounted that Sir Timothy had been in London – and presumably visiting 49 Lincoln's Inn Fields – and that, in a conversation over dinner on 17 May, John Grove's 'earnest solicitation' had persuaded Shelley to make a fresh approach to Sir Timothy without delay. This he did next day, 18 May, in a letter to his father mentioning that John Grove 'dined with us yesterday' and implying therefore that John was resuming his role as go-between.[5] It was the last such occasion.

In their entrenched positions father and son gave no ground. Harriet Shelley's hopes that 'in a week or two' she might be living at Field Place and preparing to give birth in June to a welcome grandchild were abruptly dispelled. Those earlier days at Cwm Elan in the previous spring were to be the only occasion when she slept under the roof of any of her husband's kindred.

For Elizabeth Shelley the spring of 1812 had quite the opposite significance. At the end of March she made what was probably her first visit to Ferne, where she stayed for a month before accompanying Charlotte Grove to Bath for three more weeks in each other's company.[6] Two years had passed since the cousins last saw each other, during the strangely brief visit to Field Place and the following days together at Lincoln's Inn Fields. Since then so much had happened – Charlotte's rather humiliating sojourn at Cuckfield, the publication of Elizabeth's offending poem and the strained relationship that it provoked, Bysshe's wild conduct and the family rows at Field Place. There was much to talk about if they chose to be frank with each other. At any rate, the hurt to Charlotte's pride had evidently been forgiven and dismissed.

Elizabeth would have expected Charlotte to be at Ferne but may have been agreeably surprised to find two of the brothers also –

Charles on vacation from Oxford, William waiting to join his ship, the *Scipion*. Even more surprising was the presence of Harriet, who, since her marriage, was living at Sedgehill. By chance her husband, William Helyar, had been obliged to accompany his father to London, so Harriet – now in the fourth month of pregnancy – had come to Ferne while he was away. The assembled cousins thus reconstituted exactly the little group who had walked in the romantic moonlight at Strood with Bysshe two springtimes ago. Now he, like last autumn's comet, was moving even further away and out of sight.

Elizabeth Shelley's lengthy sojourn away from Field Place – first at Bath, then at Ferne, and subsequently returning to Bath – looks like an act of policy concerted by the family elders. She was just approaching her eighteenth birthday and must surely have shown signs of the strains imposed on her by the conflict of loyalties to Bysshe and her father and by Hogg's odious advances. Even with due allowance for some exaggeration in her father's claim that Elizabeth and her mother were living in such a state of apprehension that the barking of a dog was sufficient to send them running upstairs, she certainly needed a spell in a calmer mood and less emotionally fraught circumstances. Her hostess at Bath was Mrs Parker, a name which suggests identification as Elizabeth's paternal Aunt Hellen, while her hostess at Ferne was of course a maternal aunt, Charlotte. The compassion and good sense of the long-suffering Mrs Shelley seem to show in the background of these arrangements.

At Ferne Elizabeth certainly found a sober, undemanding and even soporific atmosphere. Cousin Charlotte's love of parlour games, card games, chess and battledore set the standard indoors. Out of doors there were walks to nearby villages and viewpoints, and also Harriet's pony for Elizabeth to ride. Charlotte herself was no horsewoman but her brothers and her mother were happy to ride out with Elizabeth. In the evenings Elizabeth had her first lessons at whist. Occasionally she played cribbage and learnt another card game called Quadrille. At other times there were singing and dancing. On Good Friday she went to Berwick church with Charlotte and William. There was also a dutiful visit to be paid to her other Pilfold aunt, Bathia Jackson.

The high spirits which had marked her arrival at Ferne were not quenched by her new surroundings. On Easter Sunday Charlotte noted that politics became 'our topick [*sic*] of conversation. Elizabeth as usual permitted her Tongue its full office'. Though she might have discarded much that Bysshe had tried to inculcate in her, she evidently retained a taste for lively debate and probably for more radical notions than were current at Ferne. There seem to be echoes of Bysshe in her behaviour, including the peculiar laugh which was so characteristic of him. On 9 April Charlotte noted, 'Elizabeth not quite well before dinner. She had an hysterical laugh.'

Next day the party began to break up, when Charles returned to Oxford for the new term. On the 20th William left to join the *Primrose* sloop, off the Downs; and on the 21st Charlotte and Elizabeth set off for Bath, travelling as far as Warminster in the Grove phaeton and transferring there to Mrs Parker's carriage. Aunt Chafyn Grove was already installed at Bath, as in the previous year, and Charlotte was to stay with her while Elizabeth lodged with Mrs Parker. For the next three weeks the two girls met in the mornings to pay social calls and enjoy the fashionable amenities of Bath. In the evenings they attended routs, danced at balls and admired the actor William Betty on his return to the stage.

The time to part came after they had been constantly in each other's company for nearly eight weeks, during which a strong bond of affection had been formed and was expressed unfeignedly in Charlotte's final comment: 'Took leave of my dear Cousin with the greatest regret'. Elizabeth probably remained in Bath with Mrs Parker. If she returned to Field Place it must have been only briefly, as a letter from her that Charlotte received on 21 May conveyed the news that 'they go to Town next month'. No further correspondence is recorded until the end of November, when a gift from Elizabeth arrived at Ferne in the form of hand-painted china and card racks – a reminder of Elizabeth's continuing practice as an artist.

With her marriage to William Helyar, Harriet Grove was soon absorbed in the increasing preoccupations of maternity, bearing three children in the first three years. Charlotte's role as the supportive aunt to this young brood took her to Sedgehill for long periods. Otherwise she appeared content to be the solitary unmarried daughter whose destiny was to remain at home with her

Thomas Grove (Harriet's father, Shelley's uncle). Portrait by George Romney, 1788.

John Grove (Shelley's London host at 49 Lincoln's Inn Fields). Portrait by Margaret Carpenter, 1852.

Ferne House, 1850, as the young Groves would have known it. The original sixteenth-century building was demolished and the family seat rebuilt in 1809–11.

LEFT: *Harriet Grove,* C.*1808–9: a pencil sketch attributed to Elizabeth Shelley –* 'Elizabeth has sent me my picture' (*Harriet's diary, 29 August 1809*).

RIGHT: *An unfinished oil portrait of Shelley* C.*1822 by Amelia Curran.*

Charles Henry Grove: close companion of Shelley in London, 1811, and later rector of Sedgehill in south-west Wiltshire.

Hellen Shelley in 1862. She maintained a lifelong relationship with her Wiltshire cousins.

Field Place, the Shelleys' residence near Horsham in Sussex.

Shelley's diary, 15 January 1810: '30 copies of Zastrozzi to come – not to forget Harriet'.

Harriet's diary, 28 March 1810: 'Bysshe has sent C. & me *Zastrozzi* as it is come out'.

Shelley's diary, 1 March 1810: 'Parcel to Harriet'.

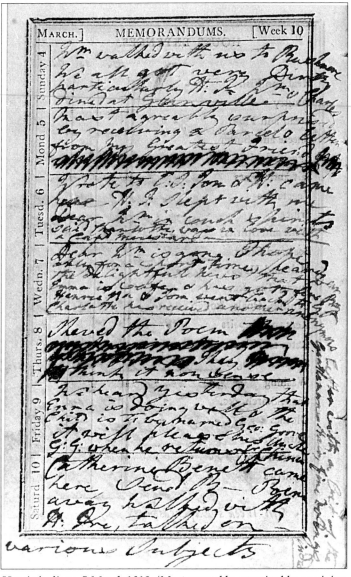

Harriet's diary, 5 March 1810: 'Most agreeably surprised by receiving a Parcel & letter from my Greatest Friend'.

'St Irvyne' (Hill Place, near Horsham): a scene of romantic memories for Shelley and Harriet Grove.

Cwm Elan: Thomas Grove's estate in Wales, where Shelley stayed in 1811 and again, with his first wife, in 1812. Painting by R. Eustace Tickell.

parents. In 1814 she made one further visit to Bath to stay with Aunt Chafyn Grove. There were the usual social events and theatre-going, but there is no mistaking the air of anticlimax. Without the stimulating companionship of sister Harriet or cousin Elizabeth that she had enjoyed in previous years, Bath had much less to offer. Evenings alone with Aunt Chafyn might be pleasant enough but hardly made the pulse beat faster.

In the first days of 1815 the death of Sir Bysshe Shelley was reported and the baronetcy passed to Shelley's father. Greater affluence as a consequence may account for Lady Shelley's decision to take her daughters annually to Bath, and to use the opportunity to visit Ferne *en route*. She arrived with Elizabeth, Margaret and Hellen on 24 May and stayed for nearly three weeks in a large house party which included Harriet Helyar and her husband. The Berwick Band was brought in to play, and on Sunday 'a large merry party' went in the barouche to Berwick church. In the following year Lady Shelley arrived with all four daughters on 24 March, accompanied from Bath by Charles Grove. When they left, Charles rode as far as Salisbury with them. In 1817 Charlotte was staying at Weymouth in August when she heard from her mother that Lady Shelley and the four girls had again been at Ferne; and in December there was news that the Shelleys were going to Bath for Christmas. Lady Shelley now had a house there, in the Circus. It had been made ready for them, with perhaps an extended stay through the winter in mind. Lady Shelley was certainly there in March 1818, inviting her sister Grove and Charlotte to visit her. In her diary Charlotte noted that 'Lady Shelley has been giving a very gay ball and supper', and added her hope that her mother would go to Bath without her – probably because Harriet was very close to a confinement and did in fact give birth two days later.

On Easter Tuesday Mrs Grove set off without Charlotte to spend a week of gaiety with Lady Shelley, attending three plays and a ball before returning with Charles to Ferne. If she brought back any news of Bysshe it was not recorded in Charlotte's diary, yet it is difficult to believe that Lady Shelley did not talk to her sister about her son's departure at that time to start a new life in Italy with Mary Godwin, whom he had married after Harriet Shelley's suicide two years earlier. Must she not have wondered if she would ever see him again?

Within weeks there came, from Bysshe apparently, a gesture of a quite baffling sort. Having seen Harriet comfortably settled with her new baby, Charlotte was next in demand to give her companionship to Tom's ailing wife Henrietta at Weymouth. Henrietta had a sad history of ill-health and it was hoped that sea-bathing would ease the pain which now made a wheel-chair necessary. During late April and May Charlotte's diary records the low-key daily life of Weymouth in these circumstances – a limited round of social calls, walks on the esplanade and games of chess – which is disturbed only once by a sentence so bizarre as to defy comprehension.

The entry for 4 May 1818, in her clear and unmistakable handwriting, at first seems likely to follow the pattern of the previous monotonous days. It reads as follows:

> Major Wallis called here. Mr Farquharson [Henrietta's brother] went to Langton. I paid morning visits with Mrs Farquharson & Henrietta. They afterwards went out in the carriage & I walked to the look-out. I played a game of chess giving a queen with Mrs F & won it. Bysshe's novel of Prometheus came.

Bysshe's novel? Prometheus? The questions multiply. By what route had the book come to Weymouth? Was it forwarded from Ferne? And was it addressed personally to Charlotte? As for its subject, the legend or myth of Prometheus had a powerful hold on Shelley's imagination and was eventually to find expression in his poem *Prometheus Unbound*; but he did not begin writing it until the autumn of 1818, four months *after* the entry in Charlotte's diary, and of course it was not a novel.

Faced with such apparent nonsense, and having a proper respect for Charlotte's sanity, I suggest that, in the cramped space remaining at the end of the day's entry, she condensed the book's *alternative* title: *The Modern Prometheus*. Its primary title was *Frankenstein*, originally published anonymously in January 1818 and rumoured at first to be the work of Shelley himself. Only later was it recognised as the work of his wife, Mary.

The manner in which this copy of *Frankenstein* or *The Modern*

Prometheus 'came' may be impersonal and prosaic in character, but Charlotte's immediate identification of it with Bysshe does recall his familiar practice in earlier years of instructing a publisher to send copies of his books to his Wiltshire cousins at Lincoln's Inn Fields or Ferne. I can only hazard a guess that in this latest case a covering note from the publisher would have mentioned the instructions of the sender and named him.

If that is so, it is the last-known link with Shelley. John Grove told Hellen Shelley that he did not meet her brother after his second marriage;[7] and Charles Henry, newly ordained, had evidently ceased to exchange letters with his cousin. Lifestyles, which had seemed so close eight years earlier, could hardly have become more widely parted.

• *Chapter Eleven* •

What was to be the last of the Shelley family visits to Ferne by Lady Shelley with her daughters took place in the spring of 1819, when the impending marriage of Bysshe's sister Mary was the dominant topic. News of it had already reached Charlotte in January, so when the Shelleys arrived just before Easter Charlotte's diary recorded, 'We had a great deal of talking'. Two days later she had a more intimate talk with Mary about 'Mr H—', the man she was to marry in June. He was Daniel Franco Haynes of Ashtead, Surrey. It is perhaps of some significance that Mary was the only one of Bysshe's four sisters to marry, and her marriage ended in divorce.

On this occasion the Shelleys stayed at Ferne for only a few days. There was an evening of dancing and another of music-making when Hellen Shelley played. And then, on Easter Saturday, they departed – though whether to Bath or to Field Place is not revealed.

A striking feature of these annual visits to Ferne and to Bath is that Sir Timothy Shelley never accompanied his family. Ferne must have become familiar to Lady Shelley and the daughters but there is no evidence in the combined diaries of Harriet and Charlotte in the decade 1810–20 that Sir Timothy ever visited it. The link between Field Place and Ferne was very much a Pilfold link. In the spring of 1821 Captain John brought his daughter Emma to Ferne. However, in the 1820s the family bonds were loosening dramatically as the young cousins matured and pursued their individual courses. Harriet became the chatelaine of Coker Court, the brothers John, William and Charles Henry married, and Ferne even saw the departure of Charlotte in 1827 when she married the fifty-year-old rector of Berwick St John, Richard Downes. A year later Mrs Grove died. The house in Lincoln's Inn Fields had other occupants: John Grove was now in full medical practice at Salisbury Infirmary and

Charles Henry had become rector of Sedgehill. The visits of John and Charles to Field Place belonged to a past epoch. The death of Bysshe by drowning in 1822 must pass without comment, as Charlotte's diary for that year is unfortunately one of two in this decade – 1827 is the other – which have not survived. The 1828 diary records the appointment in April of 'uncle Pilfold' to a command at Plymouth.

There were changes at Ferne itself. The death of Mrs Grove and Charlotte's marriage left Mr Grove alone. His son and heir, Tom, who had married again in 1824 following Henrietta's death three years earlier, was now to be installed in the great house at Ferne while his father retained the farm. Charlotte continued to visit her old home but was becoming increasingly preoccupied with her new role in Berwick St John as the rector's wife. She had always accepted 'good works' and acts of charity as a feature of her daily life, but now she had every incentive to develop her talents in this direction. She was particularly interested in encouraging thrift by a Penny Club, in arranging the subsidised distribution of coal and blankets to the poor, and in providing education for the cottagers. Eventually she succeeded in building a new schoolhouse.

It was all very different from her maiden days. Visits to balls and routs at Bath and days at the races at Salisbury and Blandford were now memories. When she travelled with her husband they were mainly intending to visit his relatives. She did, however, accompany Aunt Grove from Netherhampton to London, with her aunt's personal maidservant Vashti, in the spring of 1829. The principal object was apparently the 'electrification' of Aunt Grove by a Mr Partington, who was visited several times. Charlotte was able to see the menagerie in Regent's Park and 'Punch, a famous puppet show'; she also found time to visit several schools for young ladies at the request of sister Harriet, who wanted to send her fifteen-year-old daughter Agnes to one.

The year 1830 brought violence and tragedy to the villages of south Wiltshire when the 'Captain Swing' riots swept through the southern counties. Low wages and unemployment provoked desperate acts of arson and the destruction of agricultural machinery. Pyt House was singled out for a severe onslaught because of the hardline views of its owner, John Benett, who was a local Member of Parliament. Charlotte's account of these events, so close to Ferne and Berwick, would be particularly valuable, but again a single volume of her diary is missing. However, the tale did not end in 1830: its sequels and repercussions add the dark tones of foreboding and alarm to her account of 1831. The very first entry reveals that her brother Tom is serving on the grand jury at Salisbury where the judges are trying the late rioters. On 9 January the trials ended and she wrote, '15 to be transported that went to Pyt House'. Next night, 'Mr Farquharson has had three ricks burnt <u>of wheat</u> & 1 burnt at Piddletown. How <u>very wicked</u>!!' At the end of the month danger came even closer:

> Jan. 30. Tom came to church. They had an alarm. Two men with pistols were seen on the road about 4 in the morning Saturday who inquired of Mr Wyndham's carter if that house was not Mr Grove's of Ferne, that it looked light then but would look much lighter a few days hence. May the Almighty protect us all from these incendiaries.

There was a lull in spring and in summer harvest time before a further outbreak of violence. On 6 September Charlotte recorded 'many ricks of wheat & barley burnt at Broad Chalk' – within comfortable walking distance of the parsonage at Berwick St John; and when she went to visit Harriet next month at Coker Court the local news there was no less grim. 'The rioters have been attacking Ld. Digby's & the clergyman at Sherborne', she wrote on 29 October; and next day, 'Riots at Sherborne & Yeovil. Mr Goodford rode into the latter place & quelled the mob by his eloquence'. She returned home on the 22nd and received a letter from Harriet with the news that all at Coker were quite well, 'but have had sad riots at Yeovil & obliged to guard Coker Court & Montacute. The Yeomanry at last fired on the mob & dispersed them'.

The year continued its gloomy course to the end, with the Bristol Riots in November, a cholera outbreak in the north and finally a more personal sorrow: four days before Christmas Mr Grove received a letter from Sir Timothy Shelley. Elizabeth Shelley – 'my dear cousin' – had died at the early age of thirty-seven. It was a sad end to a life which had promised so much in her teenage years when she was fired by Bysshe's enthusiasms.

Possibly the event did something to reanimate the cousinly feelings that had been languishing. When a visit to Sussex was being considered in 1833 it was not only the fact that Charlotte's husband had a sister living in Brighton, Henrietta Downes, that stimulated their thoughts: a visit to Field Place was an added incentive. Charles Henry Grove also decided to visit Field Place at this time.

Charlotte and Richard Downes arrived in Brighton on 13 August to spend a week with his sister. What impressed them most was Brighton pier – 'the beautiful chain pier', as Charlotte described it, 'very light & elegant, painted green & hanging in festoons'. With Brighton as their base they made an excursion to stay for three nights at Field Place, where they were most hospitably received:

> My aunt & Sir Timothy Shelley most wonderful old people, the former so very like my dearest mother. Helen & Margaret played to us on the harp & piano. Elizabeth's oil paintings are very beautiful – the dining & drawing rooms furnished with them.

Next day they walked to Warnham Pond. At dinner the company included Charles Grove, 'not very well in his old complaint'. The following morning Kate Pilfold joined them. Charlotte committed a social gaffe by enquiring after Mary Shelley, apparently unaware that the marriage to Mr Haynes had come to an abrupt end when Mary eloped with a Mr Trevor.* 'I am afraid I have got into a scrape . . . heard of my cousin Mary Trevor . . . I hope that she has repented her misconduct.' When Charlotte's diary has a flurry of triple dots it is a sure sign that she is straying near the unmentionable. However, equanimity was restored and the ceremonial haunch of venison was enjoyed by all before Charlotte and Richard returned to Brighton.

During the next year, 1834, John Grove took his eldest daughter Henrietta to visit Field Place. She was the first of a new generation of Wiltshire cousins to have this direct experience of the Shelley connection. Her interest in Shelley *memorabilia* was perhaps kindled originally by this visit.†

---

* Her elopement and subsequent divorce are fully documented by Kenneth Neill Cameron in *Shelley and his Circle* II, 879–91.
† See Appendix One, pp. 135–6.

The later 1830s were a quiet period in Berwick St John and the Donheads. Charlotte's brother George died, more nephews and nieces were born, and her own energies were devoted increasingly to her Penny Club and the new school building which had sprung up under her direction with remarkable speed in 1835.

The 1840s saw the gradual closing of the principal chapter in the Grove–Shelley relationship as death began to claim the older participants, but there was a late rekindling in 1840 when Charlotte and her husband paid their second visit to Field Place. This was in August and they paused on their way at Salisbury to visit Mary Shelley – or Mary Trevor as she now was. She was living at Harnham Cottage with her second husband, 'a very gentlemanly man', and their family of three girls.

At Field Place they stayed a week. Aunt Shelley was now seventy-seven and Sir Timothy eighty-seven – both 'wonderfully well'. Hellen and Margaret were there and their younger brother John joined the party for a day's fishing at Warnham Pond. John, now the father of a family, brought his eldest son and one of his daughters with him. On other days there were visits to Mrs Medwin and to Hale to meet John Shelley's wife and their five children. To Charlotte's strict eye the children seemed so *humoured* – spoilt – 'that it is sad to witness. The eldest, Edward, the best behaved'.

In the following May Charlotte heard that Sir Timothy had received Bysshe's son Percy, now aged twenty-one. The bitter wounds were healing at last. Whether the old man liked it or not, Percy was heir to the baronetcy. He was to have an allowance of £400 a year.

Three years later, in 1844, came the news of Sir Timothy's death; and in 1846 that of Lady Shelley. Between these two events there was for Charlotte a far more painful loss, which threw the whole Grove family off balance. In November 1845 Tom Grove died. Forty men on horseback, nine carriages and three mourning coaches attended his funeral, amid consternation at Ferne as old Mr Grove, now eighty-six, found himself resuming the ownership he had given to his eldest son. Dr John Grove, as the next eldest, was persuaded to give up his medical career, to resign his post at Salisbury Infirmary and become the new master of Ferne. Tom's widow and children moved out, John's wife and children moved in, and old Thomas lived on for two more years.[1]

The biggest gap in Charlotte's testimony follows. For all ten years 1847 to 1856 her diaries are missing. When her 1857 diary takes up the threads again she is a widow and the only survivors of her generation are her sister Harriet – also widowed – and two brothers, John at Ferne and Charles Henry at Sedgehill. Bysshe's son, Sir Percy, had married a widow, Jane St John, in 1848. When his mother died in 1851 he became nominally the controlling force in the management of the literary legacy but in practice it was his wife, Lady Shelley, who undertook the presentation of an image of Bysshe that the Victorian reading public would accept and admire. While he lived, Sir Timothy had suppressed any biographical interest in his son, so the poet was fated to be damned to obscurity by his father before being sanitised to fame and respectability by his daughter-in-law; and it would not be easy to decide at whose hands he suffered the more.

The first attempt at a biography was Tom Medwin's, published twenty-five years after Shelley's death, when memories were already fading and losing precision. Ten more years passed before, in the later 1850s, a concerted effort was made to accumulate the vital testimony of his surviving circle of friends and relatives. Hogg published the two volumes of his biography in 1858 and in the same year Thomas Love Peacock began serialising his memoirs. At Boscombe Manor Lady Shelley, with the help of Bysshe's surviving sisters, was preparing her edition of *Shelley Memorials from Authentic Sources*, which she published in 1859; and it was as part of this enterprise that Hellen Shelley wrote in 1857 to John and Charles Henry Grove, asking for their recollections of Bysshe and hoping that they might have preserved some of his letters. John's contribution was determinedly lighthearted and anecdotal.[2] He had preserved no letters. Charles Henry provided a detailed and circumstantial account of the years 1810–11, which has a unique value in some respects as the only alternative to the tendentious and untrustworthy Hogg. In addition, he had preserved some letters from Bysshe. These, or some of them, he gave to Lady Shelley. On the testimony of his niece, Henrietta Hussey, he tore up others when he retired from Sedgehill in 1872.[3]

His two letters of reminiscence were written to Hellen Shelley in February 1857, when he was staying at Torquay. Bearing in mind the relatively short distance separating the Shelley establishment at Boscombe from the villages of south-west Wiltshire, there was now a convenient strengthening of the Shelley link with Ferne. In her diary in June 1857 Charlotte noted with approval the many pretty things that Hellen and Margaret Shelley had sent to the Ferne bazaar. The two sisters certainly visited Ferne during the year, and probably more than once. On 1 August Charlotte went to lunch at Ferne and met Margaret and Hellen there, together with her brothers John and Charles. At such a moment it is scarcely conceivable that they did not discuss their recent correspondence about Bysshe and Harriet Grove and the tensions and excitements of those far distant years when as children and adolescents they first began to meet each other.

Why had it all ended in the way it did? Charles's letter had hinted, with a nice blend of delicacy and vagueness, at his father's disapproval of Bysshe's subversive views. Had Harriet been torn by conflicting loyalties to Bysshe and to her father – as Elizabeth Shelley had similarly? What were the true emotions that accompanied, and precipitated, the ending of the romance?

None of them seems to have considered asking the one person still living who could speak with authority. If they did so, she refused; or they respected her confidence. Harriet remained silent. Ironically, she had been staying with Charlotte only a month before the luncheon party at Ferne. 'Time goes very fast with dear Harriet', Charlotte wrote. 'How I do enjoy my sister's dear company'. They had shared so much together that there were many topics for their conversation. If Jane, Lady Shelley, and Bysshe's sisters were among them they passed unrecorded.

There was to be no further gathering at Ferne so propitious for Shelley biography. In the following April John Grove died and a new generation succeeded. Charlotte walked to Ferne to take leave of the last of her own generation living there. Three days later she walked there again: 'The footman ushered me into the drawing room with a loud voice as "Mrs Downes". A most cordial reception from my nephew & niece. May they have many years of happiness there together.'[4]

· *Chapter Twelve* ·

By 1860 the main body of biographical material in the form of direct reminiscences by Shelley's personal circle of friends and relatives was assembled and published. The next stage was the emergence of the professional biographer, who lacked either acquaintance or kinship with Shelley, but had at least the pretension to a scholarly objectivity. Edward Dowden's two-volume *Life of Percy Bysshe Shelley*, published in 1866, opened the way to a voluminous and ever-increasing literature as each generation reassesses this major poet and incorporates any grains of fresh knowledge.

Within that context, Shelley's romance with Harriet Grove is a self-contained episode at an early stage in his development. Whatever significance it may have, it is certainly not a triviality to be brushed aside. The manner in which it has been interpreted, misreported and distorted is worth examining and correcting in the light of new information.

The early consensus of opinion was based perforce on inadequate sources. The existence of Harriet's diaries was scarcely suspected and the contents were unknown. Some Shelley letters of apparent relevance were available only after they had passed through Hogg's untrustworthy 'editing'. Charles Henry Grove's recollections were separated from events by nearly half a century. The same was true of Hellen Shelley, who was looking back to the year when she had her eleventh birthday. A further drawback is that the Grove memoir makes no reference to 1809, as in that year Charles was serving in the Royal Navy until November. It was the April visit to Field Place in 1810 that first made him aware of Shelley's feelings for Harriet. He and Shelley had not met since 1804. Medwin, Hogg and Thomas Love Peacock were aware of Shelley's first serious love affair, but only Medwin had met Harriet. Hogg did not meet Shelley until the break with Harriet was almost complete. Peacock came even later and had only hearsay evidence to offer.

From these sources a legend developed of a boy-and-girl romance which began in uncertainty as to its inception but was deeply felt by Shelley. Harriet perjured their love by disclosing to her parents the contents of Shelley's letters, which revealed his 'speculative' attitude to conventional religious values. At her father's insistence she refused to continue her correspondence with Shelley. An appeal by Elizabeth Shelley to Harriet not to be so unkind was coldly received. In the words of Lady Shelley, 'the blow fell on Bysshe with cruel force'. During the Christmas vacation in 1810 he was in the depths of despair, contemplating suicide when he learned that Harriet had married, or agreed to marry, a local farmer who was no more than 'a clod of earth'. Shelley's subsequent expulsion from Oxford finally crushed any hope of a reconciliation with Harriet.

Such is the more or less standard version in which Shelley's broken heart became the prevailing feature. What Harriet might have felt was not recorded, and it seemed legitimate to doubt if she were capable of any depth of feeling. 'As unimpassioned a damsel as may be met in a summer's day' was the gratuitous insult with which Peacock chose to dismiss her[1] – an assertion made with the surprising assurance that does sometimes accompany total ignorance.

It is to Dowden's credit that he noted the true date of Harriet's marriage, two months after Shelley's;[2] but in all other essentials the accepted narrative passed on intact to Roger Ingpen when he wrote his *Shelley in England*, published in 1917. Here again is Shelley 'suffering the tortures of unrequited love'.[3] At this date Ingpen had not seen Harriet's diaries, which he was to do later. His single quotation from them here was derived from Richard Garnett's introduction to the facsimile edition of the *Victor and Cazire* poems. It was not until 1932 that Ingpen's privately printed edition of the diaries, purchased in 1930, made it possible to correct the vagueness and distortions which had become hallowed by frequent repetition over many years.

The immediate influence of the Ingpen edition was severely limited, however. Only twelve copies were printed and they were not for sale. To what extent any of them were accessible privately to scholarly researchers I do not know,* but they certainly did not enter the mainstream of Shelley studies. It is a supreme irony that Kenneth Neill Cameron's *The Young Shelley* (1950) was written before he had seen Harriet's diaries, of which he became general editor later, supervising their publication in 1961 in *Shelley and his Circle*, volume II. For 150 years, therefore, Harriet Grove's diaries had been the vital missing factor in every attempt to describe and understand her romantic relationship with Shelley. It detracts nothing from Cameron's later magisterial reputation to record the type of misinformation that could persist as late as the 1950 publication of his early work. *The Young Shelley* asserts that in 1810 the Groves spent a week in April at Field Place, although Harriet's diary is explicit that they spent only two nights there. Her return from London is also placed in April but was in fact on 19 May; after which date 'Harriet's journal records occasional visits from a Mr William Helyer, scion of a neighbouring farming family'.⁴ It does no such thing. The Mr Helyar referred to was the rector of Tollard Royal, William's uncle, John Helyar.

Shelley and his Circle finally laid to rest errors of that kind by publishing a full annotated text of Harriet's two diaries, but inevitably there will be those tempted still to use *The Young Shelley* as a short cut to avoid reading Harriet *in extenso*.† Of the loose ends that

---

* When Newman Ivey White published his *Shelley* in the USA in 1941 he listed the Ingpen edition among his sources and also acknowledged the facility given to him by Mr Gabriel Wells, the owner of the diaries, to study Harriet's MS in the hope of restoring some of the deleted passages – a fruitless endeavour, unfortunately. His biography was not published in Britain until 1947.

† In *Shelley: the Pursuit* (London, 1974) Richard Holmes seems to have followed this course. He puts the visit to Field Place in the spring of 1809 and the forbidding of correspondence in the following autumn – at which point Harriet is said to have become 'slightly bored' with the affair. In 1810, according to Holmes, Shelley and Harriet had a second meeting at Field Place – although in fact there had been no previous visit in 1809. Thereafter 'Harriet certainly did not take the matter very seriously, and by the end of the year she had announced her formal engagement to a local gentleman farmer, William Helyer'. The misspelling of Helyer reinforces the impression that Holmes is drawing on *The Young Shelley* and adding some fictional touches of his own.

remain – among them notably Shelley's mysterious journey at the end of December 1810, and the date of Harriet's engagement to marry William Helyar – the unpublished 1811 diary of Harriet's sister is a valuable new testimony. Together with Shelley's 1810 diary, it probably represents the last contemporary material from the two families that is ever likely to be found.

Of the silent witnesses, Shelley's sister Elizabeth and Harriet's mother are the two whose words could be most revealing, but it strains the most hopeful of spirits to believe that some record of theirs still awaits discovery.

At this stage three things can be done. The first is to establish as demonstrable facts matters which have hitherto been unresolved. The second is to see what plausible conjectures can be reconciled with the established data. And the third is to consider the nature of Harriet's participation – as well as Shelley's – in what for both of them was the first experience of falling in love.

Where and when did the story begin? Medwin said it was in the summer of 1809 that they met for 'the first time since they had been children'.[5] Lady Shelley agrees. Richard Holmes opts for the spring of 1809 for this first meeting. All three locate it at Field Place. Holmes adds more positively that they had corresponded from January onwards – 'the friendship began on paper before it began in fact'.[6]

Harriet's diary makes it clear that she did not visit Field Place in spring, summer or at any time in 1809. In the spring of that year it was in London that she met Shelley. The internal evidence of her diary suggests strongly that it was not their first meeting since childhood. The manner in which she refers to Field Place and to her cousin Elizabeth Shelley gives the impression that she had seen them comparatively recently. Her nostalgic reference to the month of August 1808 reinforces the probability that she had visited Field Place then, and that the falling in love dated from that encounter, which could have included the romantic moonlit walks that were enjoyed again once more – but only once – in 1810. What is certain is that the exchange of love letters was in full flow by the end of 1808, and that on New Year's Eve her thoughts were centred on Field Place and her regret that she could not be there.

The days spent together by Bysshe and Harriet in London in 1809 throw some light on the attitudes of the parents. The initiative must have come from the Groves, who were intending to spend several weeks at Lincoln's Inn Fields and had evidently invited Mrs Shelley to come for a few days, accompanied by Bysshe. John Grove was expecting her. She did not come, however, and Bysshe alone was delivered by his father in a rather huffy manner. 'Dear Bysshe & Mr Shelley arrived here', Harriet wrote, 'the former I am very glad to see – I think Mr Shelley appears cross'. This immediate sense of Timothy Shelley as a somewhat hostile figure suggests that Bysshe may already have made Harriet aware of his potentially explosive relationship with his father. And of course it would have been Mrs Shelley, not her husband, who enjoyed the warmth of kinship with the Groves. However, Timothy Shelley mellowed later: a fortnight after his son had departed he came to dinner with the Groves and gave Harriet 'a frank for B'. As a member of Parliament he had the privilege of free postage and could give franked stationery to his personal circle. The gift of a frank was an encouragement to her to write to Bysshe at Eton.

The goodwill of Mrs Shelley towards Harriet is not to be doubted. They wrote regularly and frequently to each other. The general vitality of the correspondence between the two families is well shown in mid-July 1809 when, within five days, Harriet wrote to Mrs Shelley, Mrs Shelley wrote to Harriet and to Mrs Grove, Mary Shelley wrote to Louisa, Harriet had three letters from Bysshe and wrote to him twice, and Elizabeth Shelley wrote to John, inviting him to Field Place.

The part played by Elizabeth Shelley is particularly interesting. In the first six months of Harriet's 1809 diary Elizabeth is not mentioned. Her choice of an opposite number among her Grove cousins was John, who had stayed at Field Place during January. If they corresponded subsequently her letters to him would have been delivered to Lincoln's Inn Fields, not to Ferne, and so would have escaped Harriet's notice. In late August and early September, however, Elizabeth began writing to Harriet in most affectionate terms. Bysshe was also writing frequently at this time, so Elizabeth's letters were not a replacement for his; yet as the autumn deepened this is what they seemed to become. It was by one of Elizabeth's letters that Harriet received some new verses by Bysshe.

In this period the references to Elizabeth's letters become terse and conspiratorial. Her initials only are given: 'Heard from ES. . . . Wrote to ES', and deletions accompany them. No clear reason for this change presents itself. It is conceivable that the indignation of Felicia Hemans's mother, expressed to Mr Medwin,* had reached Timothy Shelley at this time; he might then, in his intemperate way, have restricted Bysshe's letter-writing by denying him postage franks and by plain command. One can but speculate. In December a letter from Hellen Shelley to Charlotte was noted in Harriet's diary, prompting a deletion, and a letter next day to Hellen from Harriet. The inference must be that Hellen was providing cover for Bysshe.

It is a feature of the diaries of both Harriet and her sister Charlotte that they do not enjoy the full confidence of their authors. They tend to be guarded in manner and discreet in tone, as if haunted by a fear that they might somehow fall into the wrong hands. This is to some extent because – in Charlotte's case certainly – there was a pleasure in reading it aloud to one's most intimate companion. Charlotte read passages from hers to Letitia Popham. Harriet may have behaved similarly or at least have been prepared to do so. I do not know if Regency parents had, or assumed, the right to read the diaries of unmarried daughters, but it is not impossible.

The frustration that lingers is especially pronounced in respect of Harriet's visit to Field Place in 1810. All through 1809 she had been longing to go to Field Place – at Christmas, at Easter, in the summer vacation, whenever Bysshe might be there – and she had been denied. Now in 1810 there was already agreement on a reunion at John's house in London, as in 1809, but in addition there was the real prospect that this time she would also be with Bysshe at Field Place. It should have been so straightforward. Her brothers, John, Charles, William, seemed to go to Field Place whenever they pleased.

In Harriet's case there was anxiety until the last moment, and perplexity when she did arrive. The anxiety sprang from 'some fancy' her mother had, despite the assurance that the Shelleys would be most happy to receive them. What was the nature of her mother's fancy? It is not disclosed. Nor was the reason for Harriet's perplexity. On the day the Groves arrived at Field Place she noted,

* See p. 25.

'they are all very glad to see us', but then added, 'I can not tell what to make of it. Very strange.' What was she expecting? She gives no clue, but deepens the mystery next day by writing, 'Still more odd . . . had a long conversation but more perplexed than ever'. And on the day of their departure, 'I still know not what is meant.'

Nor, alas, can we, so guarded is her response. Storm clouds of some kind among the parents seem the likeliest explanation.* There can be no suggestion of anything amiss personally between Harriet and Bysshe, since all the evidence points in the opposite direction. Charles Grove, seeing them together for the first time, considered that 'Bysshe was at that time more attached to my sister Harriet than I can express'.[7] She herself wrote, after a final walk with Bysshe and Elizabeth, of leaving 'the pleasantest party in the world'. A week later Bysshe, with his mother and Elizabeth, joined the Groves in London, and he and Harriet enjoyed what was perhaps the happiest time they ever spent in each other's company. They were together, often tête-à-tête, with the tacit approval of their parents. When they parted, Bysshe was to go to Eton for his final term; and Harriet, after a longer stay in London, was to return with her parents and brother Charles to their Wiltshire home. On two of their last three nights in London Mr Shelley dined with the Groves and was 'in great spirits'. All seemed to be well.[8]

With Charlotte staying at Cuckfield with the Pilfolds and Louisa at boarding school in Bath, Harriet depended on Charles for company at home. Sometimes he read to her – Milton and Shakespeare's *Romeo and Juliet*. What he later recalled of this period when he was exceptionally close to her was that 'in the course of that summer . . . a continual correspondence was going on, as I believe, there had been before, between Bysshe and my sister Harriet'.[9] It is not reflected as fully in her diary as might be expected, which provides a caution against the presumption that the diaries offer a comprehensive inventory of their correspondence.

There are deletions on three days in late May which can be linked with a gift of crayons that Shelley sent to her.[10] The month of June was overshadowed by the lingering and ultimately fatal illness of

---

* The tension of a quarrel between Timothy Shelley and Captain Pilfold is suggested above (see pp. 39–40).

Louisa, followed by the family visit to the seaside for a recuperative change of scene. Here Harriet recovered her spirits sufficiently to write letters to Aunt Shelley, Elizabeth and Bysshe – the loss of Louisa being the subject doubtless of her writing. August passed uneventfully until the last week when a deleted passage is followed two days later by Harriet writing to 'Percy' – not, as in July, to 'Bysshe'.

The reason for this particular exchange of letters may be that Shelley had sent the love poems he is known to have written in August. Alternatively, it may be linked with a request Shelley made to Graham at this time to buy and dispatch some books to Harriet.[11] One of the books was Sir Walter Scott's *The Lady of the Lake*, which had been attacked in Scotland for promulgating atheistical doctrines; another was Locke's *Essay concerning Human Understanding*. The significance of Locke for Shelley is best indicated by a letter Hogg wrote to Mrs Shelley after his expulsion with Shelley from Oxford, when he wanted to shrug off their joint authorship of *The Necessity of Atheism* as nothing more than the playful folly of an idle moment. Their offence amounted to no more than 'carrying perhaps a little too far some of the arguments of Locke for the amusement of a rainy morning'.[12] When Shelley later began his pursuit of Elizabeth Hitchener he sent her similarly a copy of Locke's book. It is an early indicator of the independent line of thought he had been developing during his last term at Eton and in the summer vacation of 1810. That he would want to share his new intellectual excitement with Harriet is only to be expected.

It was this shift or intensification in the tone of Shelley's letters of which Charles Grove became aware, and it is not difficult to reconstruct the new Bysshe with which Harriet was increasingly confronted, even though his actual letters are lost. When he tried to establish a correspondence with the young poet Janetta Philipps in May 1811, he told her he rejected revealed religion as the source of 'murder, war, intolerance', while he rejected natural religion 'wholly from reason.[13] I once was an enthusiastic Deist, but never a Christian'. His denunciation of sanctified murder and war became more explicit a few months later in the poem 'A retrospect of Times of Old' where a list of legal murderers in 'our own age' was added in a footnote and included Wellington and Nelson.[14] On the institution of marriage he wrote to Hogg in May 1811, 'marriage is hateful detestable, - a kind of ineffable sickening disgust seizes my mind when I think of this most despotic most unrequired fetter which prejudice has forged'.[15]

These examples, written less than a year after his disturbing letters to Harriet, probably give a fair impression of the intellectual and emotional pressure to which she was being subjected. There was little chance that she would follow Bysshe pliantly in these directions. She was, in whatever degree of devotion, a practising Christian and remained so.* With her family commitments to the Royal Navy she was unlikely to regard Nelson as less than a hero. What Shelley spoke of to Hogg as 'the indissoluble sacred union of love' was what she desired, but not 'where you have no priest but love'.[16]

I have already given my reasons, in Chapter Five, for believing that it was the insensitive publication of the poem about Charlotte which brought matters to a head and terminated the 'understanding' that had existed between Harriet and Bysshe. If Mr Grove positively forbade any further letter-writing, Harriet may not have taken it to be final and irrevocable. Would she later have returned unopened a letter from Bysshe, as Elizabeth Shelley returned Hogg's? Her response seems to have been to go into retreat and wait on events. She did not look to some new relationship for consolation.

For Shelley the situation was quite different. Going almost immediately to Oxford, he found in Hogg a friend and confidant who more than replaced the emotional union with Harriet. It is perhaps not too much to say that Oxford taught him that he had outgrown Harriet. The role of rejected lover was an attractive one to play poetically, but it was swept along on the tide of new ideas, new friendships, new potential recruits to his list of 'the good, the disinterested, the free'.[17]

The poem 'Melody to a Scene of Former Times' is a decent valedictory to Harriet.† By contrast the letters to Hogg during the

---

* Her diary for 1852 (S.R.O. DD'PH241) reveals her continuing firmness in Christian belief and practice.

† See pp. 58–60.

Christmas vacation come close to buffoonery. On 3 January Shelley wrote, 'I slept with a loaded pistol & some poison last night but did not die'; and on the 6th, 'I have been most of the night pacing a church yard'.[18] Is this more than the adoption of Gothic attitudes to impress Hogg? A main theme of the letters appears to be Elizabeth and the necessity to disabuse Hogg's mind of the belief that she would be his ideal mate in a union of love. Elizabeth's intransigence had made Shelley regret that he had ever fostered the idea, but there is the further consideration that she is in truth becoming less worthy of Hogg's regard. Her unwavering loyalty to Shelleyan ideas grows less dependable. The words usually thought to apply to Harriet, though without naming her – 'she abhors me as a Deist, as what she was before'[19] – seem more likely to refer to Elizabeth and to foreshadow Shelley's explicit disillusionment with her in April when he wrote of his sister, 'she is lost, lost to every thing, Xtianity has tainted her',[20] and in May described her as 'apathetic to all except the trivial amusements, & despicable intercourses of restrained conversation; bowing before that hellish Idol, the world'.[21] In the Christmas correspondence with Hogg the sudden outbursts about a nameless female could be associated with Elizabeth hardly less plausibly than with Harriet. Within their context the subject is Elizabeth. Harriet is never mentioned by name in these or any other letters to Hogg.

I doubt, therefore, if Shelley in the Christmas vacation was, in Ingpen's phrase, 'suffering the tortures of unrequited love'.[22] That he would cherish fond memories of Harriet is something else. Cameron pointed out astutely in *The Young Shelley* that, as the older brother of four girls, Shelley was used to having his own way and that 'the one thing that inevitably produced an extreme reaction was a serious blocking of his will'.[23] This is what he met in his two closest companions, Harriet Grove and Elizabeth Shelley, and what made Hogg seem by contrast so attractive a confidant.

To Charles Grove, spending most of his Christmas vacation at Field Place, there was very little that could be described as memorable. The state of Bysshe's feelings for Harriet was no cause for embarrassment and Charles does not seem to have been given any message to take back to Ferne or to bring with him on his return. What stayed in his memory was the journey to London with Bysshe to make the acquaintance of Miss Harriet Westbrook. It was in that direction that Shelley's thoughts were turning.

The two years of speechless bliss were over. What was their abiding essence for the two lovers? In boyhood Shelley had been ready to see himself as a future lover of ladies, but nothing suggests that he had had any significant romance before his cousin Harriet. Hellen Shelley spoke of Harriet as 'his early love'. His meetings with girls would have been limited to school holidays, and in the summer of 1808 he had only just reached his sixteenth birthday. I believe Harriet came as a heaven-sent opportunity for his first serious essay in the arts of courtship. The fact that she was his cousin eased the way. If his parents had any misgivings about his headstrong temperament they would have been soothed by the general propriety and mutual checks implicit in a cousinly relationship. The obstacle of distance meant that the deepening professions of their love for each other had to be exchanged in letters, and this was an advantage for Shelley. He was highly articulate, a born letter-writer who enjoyed formulating his feelings and his ideas on paper addressed to a single sympathetic reader. Whatever else she may have achieved, or failed to achieve, Harriet helped him to develop as a writer by matching him, letter for letter, with an ardour that matched his own. In other directions he was met with a shying away from his style of approach. She stayed with him through his novice stage as a poet and radical thinker, until the pace became too hot for her.

So volatile and insecure a lover as Shelley was too immature emotionally for a serious consideration of marriage. He had still so much to learn about himself; and of that subject he was a slow and stubborn learner. To say that he was often playing at being in love, fascinated by the thought of being in love with Harriet, is not likely to do him an injustice. The abrupt removal of her from his life would leave torn edges, but he appears soon to have found the inner knowledge that the time to part could not have been delayed much longer. The new romance was with intellectual Oxford and Hogg.

For Harriet the circumstances were quite different. She grew up in the recognition that every nice girl must have a beau. In 1808 she was seventeen. If she had had a schoolgirl 'crush' of some kind – as a remark of her brother William might perhaps imply – it is irrelevant. Her first powerful experience of love came with cousin Bysshe. At the outset she was more single-mindedly ready than he, in that, as a girl of her time, her main preoccupation would be with her future condition as a married woman, and the necessity to meet, to recognise and to win the husband on whom it depended. In the plain and honest sense of the word, for Harriet at seventeen love was her *business*. It was the area of life in which her thoughts moved most readily and searchingly. She had completed her formal education and she was confined within her family circle with no occupation to stretch her faculties and no role to play except that of marriageable daughter. Her well-bred and charismatic Etonian cousin must have appeared to her as the proverbial knight on the white horse.

The satisfaction and approval of Harriet's parents is easy to understand. Young Bysshe was in every sense 'one of them' – closely related to the Groves by marriage, heir to an estate comparable with theirs, and likely in due course to take his seat in Parliament under the patronage of the Duke of Norfolk. Only gradually could they have realised how different was the prospect that Harriet was being offered.

Of her feelings, no reader of her diaries can have much doubt. Her longing to go to Field Place, to be reunited with Bysshe there, has an intensity reminiscent of the yearning of Chekov's three sisters for Moscow. There is an inescapable poignancy in the fact that her brothers can go there so easily and tell her about it, while she can do so only if her parents escort her. And in the reverse direction – though she seems not to notice it – Bysshe never finds an opportunity to visit Ferne. What could have hindered him, had he wished to do so? He had the male freedom to travel as he pleased, and the certainty of a welcome – no less at Ferne than at Lincoln's Inn Fields or Cwm Elan. As it turned out, the few days they spent together in 1809–10 were confined to two visits to John Grove in London and a brief one to Field Place. For the rest, they waited for the mail coach.

The Harriet revealed by her own diaries and her sister Charlotte's is a girl of spirit, firm in opinion and decision. Her grief for the loss of Louisa and the haunting memory of Marianne's death by fire gave her an unusually close familiarity with tragedy at an impressionable age. Hers was not the coolly superficial butterfly temperament of self-regard that her sheltered upbringing might have produced. Her love for Shelley may have been unformed and preparatory, but its force and its sincerity come clearly through the diaries – or rather through those parts of the diaries that escaped deletion.

The remaining question, and possibly the most teasing, is the occasion and the motive for those crossings-out, which were intended somehow – but imperfectly – to erase Shelley from the record. Was it Harriet herself, in a sudden emotional gesture, who hurried through the pages, striking at each occurrence of Bysshe's name? If it were so, the likely occasion must be when she heard of Bysshe's marriage and decided the time had come for her to look to herself and make the conventional prudent marriage that would keep her securely in the family tradition. She was undoubtedly the richer for the experiences of those two years when Bysshe had been her lover. But life has to be lived on the terms it imposes.

APPENDIX ONE

The History of Harriet Grove's Diaries

Harriet Grove's diaries for 1809 and 1810 were sold at Sotheby's on 20 March 1930. The vendor was Miss Gwendolene Hussey,[1] who died in the following year. They now form part of the Carl H. Pforzheimer Collection in New York Public Library. Twelve copies, which were not for sale, were printed privately in London in 1932 with an introduction by the eminent Shelley scholar Roger Ingpen. The texts, edited and annotated by F. L. Jones under the general editorship of Kenneth Neill Cameron, were subsequently published as part of *Shelley and his Circle 1773–1822* (Cambridge, Massachusetts, 1961).

The existence of the diaries was certainly known before they came to public auction in 1930. In his *Shelley in England*, published in 1917, Ingpen quoted a key passage from Harriet's entry for 17 September 1810, referring to the *Victor and Cazire* poems.[2] Yet he also made errors of fact which he could hardly have done if he had read the diaries. For the passage quoted by him he must have been indebted to Richard Garnett, who quoted the same passage in his introduction, in 1898, to the facsimile edition of *Victor and Cazire*.

How did Garnett come by his knowledge of this excerpt from Harriet's diaries – and in whose possession were they? It is most unlikely that Harriet would have parted with them in her lifetime. I assume therefore that they were among her personal effects when she died in 1867. Her husband had predeceased her, in 1841, and much of her widowhood was spent at Montacute, the family seat of the Phelips family (Harriet's daughter, Ellen Harriet Helyar, married William Phelips in 1845). The executors of Harriet's will[3] were members of the Helyar family, with one exception – her brother, Charles Henry Grove. To him the early diaries would have had a much greater significance than to the others. There can be little

134

doubt that he took possession of them and retained them until his death in 1878.

Ingpen was aware of the link between Charles Grove and Gwendolene Hussey, whom he described as a great-niece of Harriet Grove. In a note on the *Victor and Cazire* poems he stated that her brother V. E. G. Hussey was a grandson of Charles Grove and that it was in the Hussey library that the first copy of the hitherto unknown *Original Poetry by Victor and Cazire* was found and at once issued in 1898 in the facsimile edition with Richard Garnett's introduction.[4] Garnett's ability to include the precisely apt quotation from Harriet's unpublished diary must suggest that this came from the same source, Hussey's library, with the further presumption that these documents were inherited from Charles Grove.

The Grove–Hussey connection[5] began in January 1839 when Charles's niece, Henrietta – eldest daughter of his brother John – married James Hussey, who became Mayor of Salisbury, 1843-4. They had at least six children, of whom two were boys. One of them, John, married his mother's first cousin, Agnes Grove. Agnes, born in 1841, was one of the numerous daughters of Charles Henry Grove. I have what I believe to be a photograph of the wedding party at Ferne on the occasion of her marriage to John Fraser Hussey in 1867. The children of this marriage were Victor Edwin Grove Hussey, born 1873, Gwendolene and Eleanor. I am indebted to a kinsman of theirs, E. A. Keane Ridley, for the information that Victor's career was in the Indian Civil Service, that he was living in Dorchester in 1949 but died shortly afterwards. Neither he nor his sisters married. The fact that it was Gwendolene who sold the diaries may indicate simply that she was acting for her brother.

From the foregoing it is easy to reconstruct the events of 1898. Victor Hussey, then aged twenty-five, had been examining carefully the collected books and papers of his grandfather Grove, either on his own initiative or with the prompting of his Hussey grandmother who had been taking an interest in Shelley memorabilia. The publication of John Addington Symonds's *Shelley* in 1878 had stimulated her to write three letters, now preserved in Bristol University library, in which she recounts some traditional Grove versions of episodes in the Harriet–Bysshe story and describes her exploration of the library at Ferne, which was of course her home before her marriage. In some respects Henrietta writes wildly and unreliably, but there is no reason to doubt that, for example, she found the notebook in which Shelley made notes during some chemistry lectures that he attended in 1810 with John Grove, her father, who authenticated the attribution. She was also aware of the existence of 'pocket books of my Aunt Harriet's which I can look at some day'.[6]

Hussey's discovery in 1897 of *Original Poetry by Victor and Cazire* bound up with other unrelated material would not in itself have disclosed that the pseudonyms concealed the identities of Bysshe and Elizabeth Shelley, though it had become known in 1859 that such a book had been published by Shelley. No copy of it had hitherto been found. The clinching evidence lay in Harriet's diary – in her account of the days the cousins shared together in London in April 1810, to which one of the poems refers, and in her subsequent entry for 17 September: 'Received the poetry of Victor & Cazire, Charlotte offended & with reason as I think they have done very wrong in publishing what they have of her'.[7] When Victor Hussey took the poems to John Lane in 1897 he had already seen the need to supply these relevant extracts from Harriet's diary, unless it was Richard Garnett who obliged him to do so as necessary support for the introduction that Garnett was to write. Either way, Garnett was the first Shelley scholar to learn of the whereabouts of Harriet's diaries and to see these extracts from them. If he tried to persuade Hussey to publish the diaries, or at least to make them available to scholars, he failed to do so. Another thirty-two years had to pass before their contents were known to Ingpen, and a further thirty-one years before they were made generally available, in 1961.

Valuable as they are, in the form which has survived, one cannot but bewail the impulse which scored out so many lines in an attempt to delete the references to Shelley. It is generally assumed, though without evidence, that it was Harriet herself who vandalised the diaries in this way. If it is indeed so, the question remains of when and with what motive she did it; and why she still chose to preserve the diaries in their mutilated condition.

Appendix Two

Baxter's Sussex Pocket Book, 1810

The book is bound in red, its covers and end-boards being joined with a flexible gusset to form a pocket at front and back. To allow for variations in thickness, due to the contents of the pockets, the front cover extends to form a fold-over flap with a brass clasp that can be secured in four optional positions. There is no locking mechanism but a red wax seal was applied at some time and subsequently broken. Inside the front flap a narrow sleeve is provided to contain a pencil, which is no longer there. The page size is $6\frac{1}{16} \times 3\frac{9}{16}$ inches. There are thirty-three numbered pages of a general introductory character, followed by a diary in which a week occupies one page intended for 'Memorandums', while the facing page is headed 'Cash Account' and ruled for cash entries in two columns headed 'Received' and 'Paid or Lent'.

Front endpaper: the price '3/6' is in bold figures heavily inked and apparently superimposed on a lighter form. What may have been the owner's signature is so thoroughly deleted as to be indecipherable. Lower down, in faint pencil, is 'Bill for 2 weeks £2.0.8', with a short word above 'Bill', starting with 'Ed' and presumably indicating what the bill was for.

The first leaf has been torn out leaving just enough stub to show that it carried writing. The second leaf recto is covered with bold writing which has been largely erased but is still visible and in places almost legible. Single words, e.g. 'to', can be recognised, but any coherent interpretation is very difficult, if not impossible. Verso is a coloured map of Sussex. Leaf 2 recto is the title page: 'Baxter's Sussex Pocket Book or Gentleman's County Remembrancer, being a complete annual accompt book for the pocket or desk for the year 1810', etc. 'Sussex Press, Lewes. Printed and published by J. Baxter'. The verso is blank.

Leaves 3–16 (pp. 3–30) contain a printed miscellany of useful information. Leaf 17 recto (p. 31) concludes the printed miscellany. The verso (not numbered, but p. 32) was a blank page on which a stylishly written entry reads:

Recieved [*sic*] on 22nd December 1809
From John	10 :	
From H	2 : 2 : 0
Brought over	7 : 0
	2 : 19 : 0
Hennshew (?)	1
	1
	3 : 1 : 0

Beneath this, in smaller writing, using a different pen and/or ink, but not necessarily a different calligraphy is 'Memo. due on Jan 28 – 2.0.0'.

The facing page (leaf 18 recto, numbered 33) is headed '22nd Dec. before the ensuing 1810'. It details expenditure in the same stylish and confident hand as the account of receipts on the previous page. The items are:

Edward	0 : 2 : 6
Laker	0 : 3 : 6
Graham for Pliny	2 : 15 : 0
	3 : 1 : 0

Leaf 18 verso, not numbered but p. 34, starts the diary. At this point it becomes appropriate to record each week's entries under 'Memorandum' and 'Cash Account' as a single entity, combining therefore the verso of one leaf with the recto of the next. Thus, leaf 18 verso and leaf 19 recto are described together as the week of Monday, 1 January.

Week beginning

Jan. 1   No memos. Expenditure: 'Laker 3/6, knife 4/6, Paid Taite (or Tuite) 1/0/6'. At the foot the total '1/8/6'.

Jan. 8   No memos. Expenditure: 'Brought over 1/8/6. Dancing gloves 3/6'. Total 1/12/=.

Appendix Two

Week beginning	
Jan. 15	Memo on Monday 15th: '30 copies of Zastrozzi to come – not to forget Harriet'. After 'Harriet' is what may be an ampersand and a brief deletion followed by two crosses, or kiss symbols. On Thursday 18th two words – ? Emily Sidney – have been heavily deleted. Expenditure: 'Brought over 1/12/=', which seems to have been misread. There is only one other item: 'Paid 1/1/=' but the total is given as 2/19/=.
Jan. 22	Memo on 22nd: 'Josephine – letter'. Between the two words is what may be an initial. Expenditure: 'Brought over 2/13/0 or 3/1/0. Laker for (illegible) 0/0/6. Miss M's music 1/10/0 (or 0/10/0?) Waiter 0/1/6. (No details – three dots) 0/3/6. Coach & (?) chaise 0/10/0. Layton (or Lagton) 3/6. Sally 1/0/0 Boatman (?) 10/6. Total 9/14/6'.
Jan. 29	No memos. Expenditure: balance shown as 9/14/6. 'Gloves 3/6. Two illegible items 8/6 and 8/0. 'John 1/='. Total 10/15/6.
Feb. 5	No memos. Expenditure: 'Brought over 10/15/6. Paid 2/0. man 2/0. Cakes 1/0. Bide (?) 7/6. Turnpikes 0/0/6. (illegible) 7/6. Dr G 2/2/0. Total 13/18/0'.
Feb. 12	Memos on 12th: 'Josephine . . .'. 13th the same. 'Josephine' followed by a possible initial and a word shorter than 'letter' (see 22 Jan. above). On 18th 'Zastrozzi to come out 30 copies'. Expenditure: 'Brought over 13/16/0. Coach 1/0. Ditto etc. 1/6. – Proof 5/0. Horse 7/0. (Illegible) 3/6. Total 14/14/0.
Feb. 19	A chaotic entry. A memo on 19th of four or five words (possibly 'Res . . . made vide 4 June') has been heavily overwritten by a financial statement, although the expenditure page has been left blank. The financial statement occupies the first three days' memo spaces, comprises eight items identified with single letters and totalling 18/0/3.

Feb. 26   Memo occupying Monday to Wednesday and part of Thursday: under heading 'Wandering Jew' passages from *Revelation*, Chapter 6, have been copied out. On the lower part of Thursday in much smaller writing are the words 'Parcel to Harriet'. Expenditure: no entry.

March 5   Saturday 10th: a memo of two or three words has been carefully deleted. Sunday 11th: a memo reading 'Began Wolfstein (?)'. Expenditure: no entry.

March 12   Memo on 12th: 'Deposited at Knights 7 shillings'. Expenditure 'Brought over 14/14/0 (see week of 12 Feb. above) Bottle of wine 6/6. Besants 0/0/6. Bides 0/0/6. Illegible 0/1/0. Soda water 1/=. Gloves 2/6'. Received column shows 1/1/= but it is not taken into account in the final total 15/6/0.

March 19   Memo on 20th: 'M–l–s£'. On 21st: 'Mrs.l'. The two entries seem to have been made at the same time: pen, ink and calligraphy match exactly. Expenditure shows 'Bread & cheese 1/–, Oranges 1/–, Knight 1/–, paper and pens 1/–' after an illegible item of 1/– and receipt of 16/15/– showing a credit balance of 1/4/2. No indication of where the money received came from.

March 26   One memo of two words on 28th: 'Emily today' or possibly 'Emily Sidney' but certainly 'Emily'. Expenditure: 'Dinner 10/–' and five illegible items for small amounts. Credit and debit totals are now the same: 16/15/0.

April 2   At this point the diary ceases to be used as such. There are no further financial entries and very few memo entries: none this week.

April 9   On the 10th, in tiny writing, the word 'return' – probably written at some earlier stage. Was it the date for a return from Eton? He wrote to Graham from Eton on 1 April and was at Field Place on 16 April when the Groves arrived.

Week beginning

April 16	to week beginning 28 May: Blank.
June 4	On 4th memo: 'to go to W. Wickham with Dashwood & Leslie. Resolution made'.
	On 5th the following:

EPIGRAM

J'aime un Dieu, et une jolie dame,
Une pour mon coeur, et l'autre pour mon ame.

On the cash page is written clumsily 'With — to Thirke 6 o'clock -'.

June 11 to week beginning 31 Dec.: Blank.

The leaf following the end of the diary has been cut out, apparently with scissors.

The final leaf contains publishers' advertisements: recto for a new Family Bible at the foot of which is written in large capital letters 'GOD IN HEAVEN'; verso is devoted to the British Farmer's Cyclopaedia, with no annotations.

At the foot of the endpaper is written 'W. Yates, Esq. Burlaston House, Stone, Staffordshire'.

The end pocket contains a lock of hair wrapped in a torn piece of paper inscribed with the initials 'H.G.' The hair encloses the black impression of a seal, thus:

REFERENCES

Abbreviations

UNPUBLISHED SOURCES

Shelley 1810   The 1810 diary presumed to have belonged to Shelley
                and set out here in full as Appendix Two (pp. 137–41).
                In my possession.

Charlotte Grove The diaries (or 'pocket books') of Harriet Grove's elder
                sister and close confidante, extending from 1811 to
                1858 but lacking 1822, 1827, 1830, 1838 and 1847–56.
                In my possession.

WRO 1641   Grove family papers in the Wiltshire Record Office,
                Trowbridge.

SRO-DD/WHh61   Helyar family papers in the Somerset Record Office,
                Taunton.

PUBLISHED SOURCES

Medwin   Thomas Medwin, *The Life of Percy Bysshe Shelley* (1847;
                ed. H. B. Forman, 1913).

Hogg   Thomas Jefferson Hogg, *The Life of Percy Bysshe Shelley*,
                2 vols. (1858). All references are to the 1933 edition,
                ed. Humbert Wolfe, which also includes Thomas Love
                Peacock's *Memoirs*.

Letters   F. L. Jones (ed.), *The Letters of Percy Bysshe Shelley*, 2 vols.
                (Oxford University Press, 1964). All references are to
                Vol. I, giving date and number. Where an original
                lacked a date I have accepted Dr Jones's provisional
                dating. I am indebted to his copious and valuable
                annotations for much supplementary information.

Esdaile   Kenneth Neill Cameron (ed.), *The Esdaile Notebook*
                (1964). Shelley's collection of his early poems. Camer-
                on's commentary is particularly illuminating for the
                period of most relevance to the present book,
                1809–11.

References

HG   The diaries or 'pocket books' of Harriet Grove for the years 1809–10. Date of entry given for each reference. Twelve copies printed privately and not for sale in 1932 (London) with introduction by Roger Ingpen. The standard text is in Vol. II of *Shelley and his Circle*, ed. Kenneth Neill Cameron (Carl H. Pforzheimer Library, New York; Harvard and Oxford University Presses, 1961).

CHG   Charles Henry Grove's early recollections of Shelley, communicated in 1857 to Hellen Shelley in correspondence and published in Hogg's biography, to which references are made.

Shelley in England   Roger Ingpen, *Shelley in England* (London, 1917).

Young Shelley   Kenneth Neill Cameron, *The Young Shelley* (London, 1951).

Dowden   Edward Dowden, *The Life of Percy Bysshe Shelley* (London, 1886).

Victor and Cazire   Richard Garnett (ed.) *Original Poetry; by Victor and Cazire* (Worthing, 1810; facsimile London, 1898).

Shelley and his Circle   See *HG* above. In addition to the text of Harriet's diaries, Vol. II contains much other relevant material, notably evidence of Hogg's editorial corruptions.

Other published sources are given, with full title, in context.

Chapter One

1. The family seat of the Groves was Ferne. The alternative forms *Ferne* and *Fern* were adopted or discarded at will by successive generations. The modern standard is Ferne. The house and its surrounding park were set in a cluster of villages in south-west Wiltshire – Donhead St Andrew, Donhead St Mary, Berwick St John and Tollard Royal – close to the Dorset town of Shaftesbury.
2. Burke's Peerage and Baronetage, 1897. *Dowden*, p. 3.
3. For a fuller account of the Grove family history, see the unpublished Grove archive, *WRO 1641*; also my *Cranborne Chase* (London, 1980), pp. 154–9, and *Concerning Agnes* (Gloucester, 1982), *passim*.
4. For information about the White and Pilfold families I am indebted to Surrey Local Studies Library, Guildford; to James Bieri, *in litt*; and to M. O'Connor, *History of Effingham* (Effingham, 1973).
5. Poole, *Burke's Extinct and Dormant Baronetcies*, and *Medwin*, p. 13.
6. *HG*, 7 May 1810.
7. *DNB*.
8. *CHG* in *Hogg*, II, p. 154, and *Medwin*, p. 13.
9. *CHG* in *Hogg*, II, p. 154.

References

10. Ibid.
11. *HG*, 24 November 1809, and 13 December 1809.
12. *Esdaile*, pp. 171–2.
13. Ibid.
14. Ibid., pp. 306–7.
15. Sir John Rennie, *Autobiography* (1875), pp. 1–2, cited *Young Shelley*.
16. *Shelley in England*, pp. 42–3.
17. O'Byrne, *Naval Biographical Dictionary* (1849).
18. Michael Millgate, *Thomas Hardy* (Oxford, 1982), p. 125.
19. *Esdaile*, pp. 308–9.
20. *HG*, 6 March 1809.
21. Harrow school records.
22. *WRO 1641*. When, as Philippa Long, she married John Grove her dowry was £2000. When her son Thomas married she leased the manor house at Netherhampton, near Salisbury, from the Earl of Pembroke and lived there with her daughter Philippa, who inherited Netherhampton and is identified in Harriet's diaries as 'Aunt Grove'. The house passed eventually to Harriet's brother William.
23. A. Henry-Higginson, *The Meynell of the West* (London, 1936), *passim*.
24. C. W. Newman, *Transactions of the Radnorshire Society*, vol. XXX (1960).
25. *Charlotte Grove*, 20 April 1828: 'The funeral of Robin King 82. He went into Wales with us when my father lived at Cwm Elan in Radnorshire'.
26. *WRO 1641*. There is the further possibility that Thomas Grove senior occupied the house originally, in the 1790s.
27. *Charlotte Grove*, 14 September 1814.

Chapter Two

1. The family seat of the Portmans was Bryanston, adjacent to Blandford Forum. The New Year's ball seems to have been an annual event at Blandford. The Groves who attended it stayed overnight at Bryanston as the Portmans' guests.
2. *Charlotte Grove*, 30 August 1817: 'Sir Richard Glynn, my father & brothers went to Salisbury to vote for John & he was elected Physician of the Hospital'. He was re-elected annually until 1845 when the death of his elder brother obliged him to resign and prepare to inherit Ferne from his aged father.
3. Mr Wake was not Harriet's favourite man; see *HG*, July 1809.
4. As heir apparent to Ferne, Tom Grove had little incentive to establish a 'seat' of his own. The Welsh estate, Cwm Elan, was given to him and was used as a summer residence. At other times he and Henrietta occupied houses owned by her father. At Tarrant Gunville Mr Farquharson owned what remained of the vast palace that Vanbrugh had created for Bubb Dodington, Lord Melcombe. Tom and Henrietta probably occupied some part of the Eastbury estate.
5. *Charlotte Grove*, 3 January 1811.

6. Hellen Shelley in *Hogg*, I, p. 27.
7. Harriet's paternal grandmother was Philippa Long, whose younger sister Elizabeth married Edward Rudge (1717–90) of Salisbury and Bath (*Burke's Landed Gentry*). From the seventeenth century the Longs were prominent in the public and parliamentary life of Wiltshire and Hampshire. Their memorials include two sculptures by Flaxman in Salisbury cathedral.
8. Walter Long of Preshaw (b. 1788–1871) married Lady Mary Carnegie on 12 February 1810 (*Burke's Landed Gentry*).
9. Letter from Shelley to James T. T. Tisdall. *Letters*, 7 April 1809 (No. 6).
10. *HG*, 19 April 1809.
11. Lower Donhead was an alternative name for Donhead St Andrew. The two Donhead villages form a continuous whole, with Donhead St Mary known as Upper Donhead.
12. Little Park was the seat of John Waddington near Wickham, Hampshire. There is no trace of the mansion, which is now replaced by a modern industrial estate.
13. *Medwin*, p. 18.
14. *Charlotte Grove*, 19 August 1833.
15. *CHG* in *Hogg*, II, p. 155.
16. Ibid.
17. Rev. John Helyar owned Dove's Mansion House at Tollard Farnham and another smaller property there, described as 'late Harvey's' (auctioneer's particulars, 1815: *WRO 1641*).
18. Sources include Helyar family archive, *SRO–DD/WHh61*; *Burke's Landed Gentry*; *HG* and *Charlotte Grove* (many diary entries); Tollard Royal parish register; Grove family archive *WRO 1641*; John Collinson, *History of Somerset* (1791).
19. O'Byrne, *Naval Biographical Dictionary* (1849).

Chapter Three
1. *Medwin*, pp. 58–9.
2. Rev. John Tregonwell Napier (1785–1819). His name appears in the Tollard Royal register as deputy for John Helyar in 1810, the year in which he also became rector of Chettle. There is a memorial tablet to him in Chettle church.
3. *Shelley 1810*, 1 March.
4. *Medwin*, p. 49.
5. *Shelley 1810*, pp. 190–1.
6. *Medwin*, p. 49.

Chapter Four
1. *CHG* in *Hogg*, II, p. 154.
2. *Letters*, 1 April 1810 (No. 8).
3. Ibid.

References

4. Ibid., 23 April 1810 (No. 10).
5. *CHG* in *Hogg*, II, p. 155.
6. *Letters*, 29 May 1810 (No. 12).
7. *CHG* in *Hogg*, II, p. 155.

Chapter Five
1. *Victor and Cazire*, pp. unnumbered.
2. Ibid, pp. 24–5.
3. Ibid., pp. 33–4.
4. Ibid., pp. 35–6.
5. *HG*, 19 May 1810.
6. *Victor and Cazire*, pp. 10–13.

Chapter Six
1. *CHG* in *Hogg*, II, p. 155.
2. Ibid.
3. Lady Shelley (ed.), *Shelley Memorials from authentic Sources* (1875; first published 1859), p. 13.
4. Ibid.
5. *Charlotte Grove* 3 October 1811 – a fact hitherto unknown.
6. *Letters*, 14 March 1812 (No. 175).
7. Joseph Gibbons Merle, 'A Newspaper Editor's Reminiscences' (*Fraser's Magazine*, June 1841), cited R. Holmes, *Shelley, the Pursuit* (London 1974).
8. *Letters*, April 1811 (No. 65).
9. *Hogg*, I, p. 28.
10. *Letters*, 20 December 1810 (No. 30).
11. *Medwin*, p. 39.
12. *Letters*, 26 March 1809 (No. 5).
13. *Medwin*, p. 39.
14. *Shelley 1810*, entry of 26 February.
15. *Letters*, 28 September 1810 (No. 19).
16. *Medwin*, p. 39.
17. *Letters*, 20 December 1810 (No. 30).
18. Ibid., 20 December, 1, 3, 6 and 11 January 1810 (Nos. 30, 34, 35, 36 and 38).
19. Roger Ingpen (ed.), *Complete Works of Shelley*, Vol. 8 (1965), p. 39 n., cites Peacock as proposing that 'She is married' should read 'She married!' – with the inference of a future commitment to marriage, following a newly announced betrothal. As a matter of record there was no such betrothal and the words Shelley wrote are 'she is married'. Whether he intended to write something different or may not have been referring to Harriet are interesting speculations only.
20. *Hogg*, I, pp. 96–7.
21. Sotheby's, 30 June 1948, cited *Shelley and his Circle*, II, p. 671.

22. Ibid., p. 670.
23. Ibid., p. 672, and *Letters*, 23 December 1810 (No. 31).

Chapter Seven
1. *Letters*, 18 December 1810 (No. 28), footnote 1.
2. Ibid., 2 December 1810 (No. 27).
3. *CHG* in *Hogg*, II, p. 155.
4. *HG*, 28 December 1810, and *Charlotte Grove*, 5 January 1811.
5. *Letters*, 18 December 1810 (No. 28).
6. *HG*, 28 and 31 December 1810, and *Charlotte Grove*, 1 January 1811.
7. *CHG* in *Hogg*, II, p. 155.
8. *Letters*, 1 January 1811 (No. 34).
9. Ibid., 6 January 1811 (No. 36).
10. *HG*, 31 December 1810.
11. *Charlotte Grove*, 1 January 1811. Incidentally, Charlotte spells Lyttleton with a 'y', while Harriet and the Ordnance Survey preferred Littleton.
12. *Young Shelley*, pp. 334–5, and *Shelley and his Circle*, II, p. 682.
13. *Letters*, 11 January 1811 (No. 38).
14. Ibid., 20 December 1810 (No. 30).
15. Ibid., 6 January 1811 (No. 36).
16. Ibid., 11 January 1811 (No. 38).
17. See Chapter 6, note 19.
18. *Charlotte Grove*, 3 October 1811.
19. *Charlotte Grove*.
20. Ibid.
21. Ibid.

Chapter Eight
1. *Letters*, 17 January 1810 (for 1811) (No. 42), and 20 January 1811 (No. 43). *CHG* in *Hogg*, II, p. 155. St Bartholomew's Hospital Archives, G54, p. 315.
2. *Letters*, 11 January 1811 (No. 37).
3. Ibid., 28 October 1811 (No. 128).
4. *Charlotte Grove*.
5. *WRO 1641*.
6. *Charlotte Grove*.
7. Ibid.
8. *Hogg*, I, p. 178.
9. Ibid., p. 180.
10. *CHG* in *Hogg*, II, p. 156.
11. Ibid., p. 157.
12. Ibid., p. 156, and *Letters*, 8 October 1811 (No. 114).
13. *Letters*, 18 April 1811 (No. 59).
14. Ibid., 24 April 1811 (No. 61).
15. Ibid., 28 April 1811 (No. 63).

16. John Grove in *Hogg*, I, pp. 196–7.
17. *Letters*, 24 April 1811 (No. 61).
18. *Shelley in England*, pp. 230–1.
19. *Letters*, 29 April 1811 (No. 64).
20. Ibid., 26 April 1811 (No. 62).
21. Ibid., 28 April 1811 (No. 63).

Chapter Nine
1. *Letters*, 12 May 1811 (No. 69), and 14 May 1811 (No. 70).
2. Ibid., 21 May 1811 (No. 76).
3. Ibid.
4. Ibid., 16 May 1811 (No. 73), and ? May 1811 (No. 74).
5. F. L. Jones, *Letters* (footnote to No. 73).
6. *Letters*, 3 December 1812 (No. 211).
7. *Charlotte Grove*, May and June 1811.
8. *Letters*, ?10 July 1811 (No. 92).
9. George Nicholson, *The Cambrian Traveller's Guide in Every Direction* (1813); C. W. Newman, 'Notes on Cwm Elan' (Radnorshire Society's *Transactions*, Vol. XXX, 1960); D. Hawkins, 'The Groves of Cwm Elan' (Radnorshire Society's *Transactions*, Vol. LV, 1985).
10. George Gilfillan (ed.), *The Poetical Works of William Lisle Bowles* (Edinburgh, 1855), Vol. I, pp. 115–25.
11. *Esdaile*, pp. 77–8.
12. *Letters*, ?13 July 1811 (No. 93).
13. Ibid., ?13 July 1811 (No. 94).
14. Ibid., ?10 July 1811 (No. 92).
15. Ibid., ?28 July 1811 (No. 101).
16. Ibid., ?13 July 1811 (No. 93).
17. Ibid., ?15 July 1811 (No. 96), ?22 July 1811 (No. 97), ?25 July 1811 (No. 98), and ?28 July 1811 (No. 101).
18. Ibid., ? July 1811 (No. 95).
19. Ibid., 26 July 1811 (No. 100).
20. Ibid., ?22 July 1811 (No. 97).
21. *Hogg*, I, p. 181.
22. *CHG* in *Hogg*, II, p. 156.
23. *Letters*, ?3 August 1811 (No. 103).
24. Ibid., ?14 August 1811 (No. 105).
25. Ibid., 15 August 1811 (No. 106).
26. *Charlotte Grove*. Flora Long, a daughter of Richard Godolphin Long, MP, of Rood Ashton, Wiltshire, counted the poet George Crabbe among her admirers. He referred to her as his 'sweet friend' (Thomas C. Faulkner (ed.), *Selected Letters and Journals of George Crabbe* (Oxford, 1985)).
27. *Charlotte Grove*.
28. *CHG* in *Hogg*, II, pp. 156–7.
29. *Charlotte Grove*, 6 September 1811: 'On Friday night, September 6, its

right ascension was by three observers placed at 159 degrees, and its declination North at 41 degrees . . . for common observation the best instrument is an opera-glass' (*Gentleman's Magazine*, September 1811).
30. *Charlotte Grove*, 3 October 1811.
31. *Shelley in England*, p. 337.
32. Ibid., pp. 347–8.
33. *Letters*, 21 October 1811 (No. 121).
34. Ibid., 29 October 1811 (No. 129).
35. Ibid.
36. *Charlotte Grove*, 14 November 1811. The ceremony was performed by Bathia Pilfold's husband, Rev. Dr Gilbert Jackson, rector of Berwick St John. The Jacksons' daughter Fanny was one of the bridesmaids, the others being Harriet's sister Charlotte, her niece Emma Waddington and her friend Helen Tregonwell. No other details are given.

Chapter Ten
1. *Letters*, 26 November 1811 (No. 145 and note).
2. *CHG* in *Hogg*, II, p. 157.
3. *Letters*, 25 April 1812 (No. 180).
4. Ibid., 7 June 1812 (No. 192, note).
5. Ibid., 18 May 1813 (No. 236 and note 3).
6. Pp. 108–13 based on *Charlotte Grove*, diaries.
7. John Grove in *Hogg*, I, p. 197.

Chapter Eleven
1. *Charlotte Grove*, and *WRO 1641*.
2. John Grove in *Hogg*, I, p. 197.
3. Irving Massey (ed.), 'Some Letters of Shelley Interest' (*Keats–Shelley Memorial Bulletin*, No. XIX, p. 16, 1968). The letters are in Bristol University Library.
4. *Charlotte Grove*.

Chapter Twelve
1. Thomas Love Peacock, 'Memoirs of Percy Bysshe Shelley', *Fraser's Magazine*, 1858–60; reprinted in *The Life of Percy Bysshe Shelley*, ed. Humbert Wolfe (London, 1933).
2. *Dowden*, p. 101 footnote.
3. *Shelley in England*, p. 143.
4. *Young Shelley*, pp. 14–15.
5. *Medwin*, p. 47.
6. Richard Holmes, *Shelley: the Pursuit* (London, 1974), ch. 1, p. 28.
7. *CHG* in *Hogg*, II, p. 154.
8. *HG*. All references pp. 124–7 are to Harriet Grove's diaries.
9. *CHG* in *Hogg*, II, p. 155.
10. *Letters*, 29 May 1810 (No. 12).

11. *Ibid.*, 11 August 1810 (No. 14).
12. *Ibid.*, 23 June 1814 (No. 89, footnote 2, lines 33–5).
13. *Ibid.*, ?May 1811 (No. 74).
14. *Esdaile*, p. 97.
15. *Letters*, 8 May 1811 (No. 67).
16. Ibid. and 4 June 1811 (No. 80).
17. *Letters*, 28 October 1811 (No. 128).
18. *Ibid.*, 3 January 1811 (No. 35) and 6 January 1811 (No. 36).
19. *Ibid.*, 3 January 1811 (No. 35).
20. *Ibid.*, 28 April 1811 (No. 63).
21. *Ibid.*, 21 May 1811 (No. 76).
22. *Shelley in England*, p. 143.
23. *Young Shelley*, p. 15.

Appendix One
1. Ingpen (ed.), *The Journal of Harriet Grove* (privately printed, London, 1932), p. vi. The buyer at the auction was Gabriel Wells.
2. *Shelley in England*, p. 98.
3. SRO.DD/WHh61.
4. Roger Ingpen & Walter E. Peck (ed.), *The Complete Works of Percy Bysshe Shelley* (London, 1965), Vol. I, p. 413.
5. *WRO 1641*.
6. See Chapter 11, note 3.
7. *HG*, 17 September 1810.

INDEX